SATAN WITH HIS ANGELS WERE THROWN DOWN TO EARTH

REV 12:9

LUCIFER REBELLION

CHRIST VS SATAN - FINAL BATTLE FOR EARTH HAS BEGUN

TRINITY ROYAL

CHRIST VS SATAN - FINAL BATTLE FOR EARTH HAS BEGUN

LUCIFER REBELLION

TRINITY ROYAL

Library of Congress Control Number: 2022915216

CONTENTS

Special Bonus – Free books to our readers

Free books to our readers

War in Heaven came to Earth. Satan Rebellion:

https://dl.bookfunnel.com/ea12ys3dmk

Your Life in Heaven:

https://dl.bookfunnel.com/vg451qpuzs

"And there was **war in heaven**: Michael and his angels fought against the dragon; and the dragon fought and his angels, And prevailed not; neither was their place found any more in heaven.

And the great dragon was cast out, that old serpent, called the **Devil, and Satan, which deceiveth the whole world: he was cast out into the earth, and his angels were cast out with him.**" – Revelation 12: 7-9

INTRODUCTION

All the major religions of the world including Christianity, Islam, Judaism, Hinduism, and Buddhism agree on one critical fact – there is Heaven and hell, God and His adversary, Light and Dark, and both are opposites. The adversary is called by different names including Satan, Shaytan, Iblis, and Lucifer. All religions also agree both factions are powerful adversaries and that Human beings are part of this epic battle. Most of the details in all of the scriptural texts are either high-level or sketchy at best, there is no explanation. This is subject to different interpretations and confusion among theologians.

The Holy Bible when seen through the lens of history has more info comparatively than other religious scriptures about the war in heaven but this also falls short. My sincere attempt in this book is to shine a light on this great epic war that has origins beyond planet Earth space and time. The reader will travel back in time when Lucifer Rebellion began. We will see what exactly happened at that time, and since then, and its effects on this present day.

To my knowledge, this is the first time this level of information is being presented to Humanity. Because it is TIME. The final bell has rung, and the climatic battle is at hand. You will see why this is so later in the book.

The Matrix was one of the most popular movies ever released in the history of the industry. Just about anyone, anywhere in the world, can describe its basic plot to you: The hero, Neo, an ordinary computer programmer, somehow knows that something is off in the world he inhabits. He meets Morpheus, takes the red pill, and realizes that his world is an illusion—one created by sentient machines to enslave humanity so that humans could be used as a power source by malevolent mechanisms. By breaking free of the matrix, the illusory world, Neo could lead his fellow man to freedom and liberation.

Now think of a different scene, one not portrayed in that movie or any other. Imagine one army on the right side of a great galactic battlefield—a mighty host of creatures of all shapes and sizes, hoisting aloft a banner consisting of three concentric unbroken azure circles (representing the good government of the entire universe) on a white background. At the head of this army of Light is the greatest religious figure we know of—Jesus Christ. Opposing him, streaming from the left side of the galactic battlefield, are legions upon legions of Dark creatures, as varied as their Light counterparts but wreathed in shadow and ill omen. The most notorious demon in history, Satan, is leading them, carrying a banner displaying a red circle on an equally white background with a solid black circle in its center.

Surrounding these great armies is a galactic host of trillions upon trillions of creatures. Not only from our galaxy but from across the entire universe; they are watching the two forces of Light and Dark go head-to-head with each other. At the very center of the struggle between them is a single little ball of blue and green: Our home planet, earth. And this battle is the very climax of a struggle that has been going on for far, far longer than any of us has been alive. This battle takes place at the 11th minute of the 11th hour of the great war between these elemental forces, with the Earth and Universe at stake.

The armies cannot fight on, or interfere with Earth directly on their own. But the residents of the earth have free will and can petition the warriors of both sides for help, depending on their freely made choices. The two sides are fighting for the souls of humans and will lead them to either destruction or ascension to Heaven.

Questions this Book Will Answer

Book-1:

- What is Lucifer's Rebellion? When and why did the Lucifer rebellion start?

- What is Lucifer/Satan's agenda?

- How did the 'Fall' happen?

- What is the ONE reason Dark and Light are fighting for on planet Earth?

- Why did God have to make a clarion call to all the angels for humanity's assistance?

- How the Dark and Light are fighting and what is the evidence?

- What is the reason for the bestowal of the Creator of the Universe on Earth - Jesus Christ?

- What exactly happened between Christ and Satan in the wilderness on Mt. Hermon?

- What is the evidence that we are almost at the climatic battle point, at the 11th hour and 11th min?

- How do dark forces operate to keep you stuck in this Veil of separation (spiritual Matrix)? How do you know or even recognize this?

Book-2:

- How to free yourself from the Matrix?

- What did Christ accomplish in His First Coming?

- What is on the agenda for His Second Coming? (hint: It is more than rapture)

- What can planet Earth expect from Christ's Second coming?

- When can we expect the Second Coming event?

- How long do we have? When is this epic war going to end?

- What exactly happens at the end of the war?

Hmm...these are really good questions. Do you agree? This book will answer all these and much more.

This will revolutionize the way you see life.

"God's laser focus is on Earth and humanity; this is where all the action of the universe is. Big shots from across the universe are gathered and watching the chess games being played by Light and Dark armies. This is our current reality, not fiction." – Trinity Royal

WHO THIS BOOK IS FOR?

THE MATRIX HAS YOU...

"Tis strange-but True; for Truth is always Strange, Stranger than Fiction" – Lord Byron

Before we begin, I must make clear who this book is for and who it is not for, what you can gain from it, and what sorts of things you will not find inside it.

What this book is NOT:

- This book is NOT for people who do not believe in God, Christ, Angels, Spirits, or Heavenly realms of existence to which human souls can progress after death sleep

- This book is NOT for people who do not believe in the existence of Heaven or Heavenly worlds, or other material and non-material worlds

- This is not an academic book about religion. It does not discuss the Bible teachings or any other religious teachings specifically, says nothing about translation or hermeneutics or similar subjects, and so on. This book will draw upon religious ideas from a variety of religious sources to illuminate higher truths—but to analyze the texts themselves is beyond its scope.

- By the same token, this book does not aim to discredit the teachings of any religious book or tradition. It will quote passages from the Bible when necessary.

- This book is NOT fiction or fantasy! While I do not claim to know everything, it is based on many years of painstaking research, as well as knowledgeable sources who are part of spiritual warfare

- This book is NOT for atheists or those who do not believe they have a greater place within the workings of the universe

- This book is NOT for people who have consciously chosen the Dark side. You have already made your choice, and you will only bring negative energies into the world or to this book

- If you are closed-minded, and just want to find faults; you will miss the big picture. This is NOT for you.

So, who is this book for?

- For those who want to know about Lucifer Rebellion

in Heaven

- For those who have gaps in their scripture knowledge and are looking to fill in some knowledge gaps related to War in heaven

- For those who want to know about God, Christ, Lucifer, and Satan

- For those who what to know how Dark and Light operate in the world and what their ideologies are

- For those who want to know if there is a war in heaven and earth and if it real

- For those who need proof of war being fought

- For those who what to know why God has sent Christ to planet Earth

- For those who want to know the primary objective(s) for Christ's First Coming

- For those who want to know why you are not able to interact directly with God and Angels

- Why you are powerful and why both dark and light have vested interest in your soul

- People who are confused about life and why darkness exists on Earth

- People who want to know why God does not interfere directly in the world and put an end to all human suffering

- Knowledge seekers and historians. Guaranteed to be enlightening

- Those who want to understand the "big picture" of human existence

- Those who have a deep sense that something is wrong with the world and you cannot put your finger on it

If you are a member of one of the latter groups, prepare yourself.....this might just change your life.

YOUR JOURNEY BEGINS – DOWN THE RABBIT HOLE

Fasten seat belts, please...

Prepare for lift-off...

Let's travel back in time to 200,000 Earth years to the beginning of the Lucifer Rebellion

Journey Begins

"You are here because you know something. What you know you can't explain, but you feel it" - *Morpheus*

Down the rabbit hole, we go...

Main Characters

Before we dive deep, let us see who the main characters are. We will get to know more about all of them in the following chapters. The names of heavenly beings are usually quite long and are usually sung with intricate syllables and phonetics. For our understanding, the following will suffice.

GOD - The Father, Creator of everything seen and unseen

Christ or Jesus Christ - The names are used interchangeably in this book. Christ is the "Son of God". He is the field commander of all light forces in the Universe. Christ is the creator of our Universe and is the one who was born as a baby in Bethlehem on Earth named Jesus. Christ is the name of this great being. Christ also has a title called Michael in Higher universal realms.

Arch Angel Michael – Arch Angel Michael or ark angel Michael is local to our Universe and is often confused with the title Michael that Christ has mentioned in Bible. This Arch Angel is NOT part of the Lucifer rebellion which mostly happened outside of our Universe. Arch Angel Michael is local to our universe. This arch Angel is popularly also called the Angel of Resurrection.

Lucifer – Lucifer was created by God as a unique being, the most beautiful angel of all created, and he had free will, and the ability to make his own decisions and act on them.

Satan – Satan is a powerful heavenly being, so much so that he was specifically chosen by Lucifer to be his ultimate trump card during the war in heaven. Next to both Christ and Lucifer, he is the most powerful angel created by God. Satan was more noble, just, and fair but strict and firm. He was an exalted cherub and thus had great pride over his power and position.

Caligastia - The planetary prince of Earth at the time of the fall of Earth to Lucifer's rebellion. He remained in power until Christ walked on Planet Earth.

CLIMATIC BATTLE SCENE ON EARTH: CHRIST VS LUCIFER

T here's no turning back now—you're as ready as you will ever be.

As Morpheus told Neo in The Matrix, "You take the blue pill, the story ends, you wake up in your bed and believe whatever you want to believe. You take the red pill, you stay in Wonderland, and I show you how deep the rabbit hole goes. Remember, all I'm offering is the truth. Nothing more."

The curtain is rising on the greatest show the entire universe has ever seen. You have the front seat.

You now behold a great battlefield where two armies are facing off against each other, each of which is millions upon millions of soldiers strong. One of these armies consists of golden spirits bathed in heavenly alabaster light. At its head is the banner of Christ: The banner for this army of light is set of three concentric azure circles on a pure white background, representing the Holy Trinity of creation (Universal Father, Eternal Son, and Infinite Spirit).

The other army is made up of horrifying monsters and shadowy beings. At the head of this army is the most horrible monster of them all, the fallen angel Lucifer, determined to enslave all of creation, and mire the entire universe in darkness for all eternity. Lucifer carries his banner. It has a white background, like that of Light, but in its center is a single red circle, and in the center of that is a single solid black circle. Some say it looks like a terrible eye; some seekers might compare it to the eye of Sauron from the Lord of the Rings movie trilogy. Many times even entertainment can reveal hidden spiritual truths, for just like Sauron in Tolkien's books, Lucifer is a cruel dominator who wants to control everyone and everything else.

These two armies of Light and Dark are utterly dwarfed by the spectators surrounding them. A great throng of angels in the entire universe is watching the confrontation intently. But the real center of attention is between those two massive armies. Both of them are vying for a single small ball of rock—a pale blue dot, as Carl Sagan might say. On this pale blue dot live billions of humble material creatures, that evolved throughout millions of years, the vast majority of which are completely unaware of the struggle being waged around them and their central significance to it.

You guessed right—that pale blue dot is Earth, and its residents, human beings—including you and me—are the true prize of this conflict. The forces of Light, led by Christ in his human form as Jesus Christ, want the best for humanity. They want us to liberate ourselves from the Veil which keeps us ignorant of spiritual warfare and higher realities so that our souls can ascend to Heaven and reach closer and closer to God. Lucifer's army wants to enslave us or annihilate us if that is not possible. He wants to stunt our spiritual development and keep us blind, miserable, and in perpetual conflict with each other. While the Light gains energy from human beings purifying their souls, ascending to higher vibratory planes after death, and turning evil to good, the Dark gains energy from trapping souls in the material universe forever, so their negative emotions can be used as batteries powering Lucifer's evil plans.

Despite the intensity of this spiritual war, there are some rules both sides have to accept. There is a veil of separation that exists between the seen and unseen realms of Heaven. We will see in later chapters why this Veil or Matrix came into place. There is war in the unseen that most of humans have very little understanding of, yet this is what has shaped Earth and Human existence. We will look "behind the veil" in future chapters.

As the curtain rises, the great archangel Gabriel, popularly known as the messenger of the highest, has blown his war horn. The eyes of the entire universe are on Earth—and YOU, specifically! God and all of His creations are paying very close attention to your choices and actions. However, they are not judging you one way or the other—you are perfectly free to make all of your own choices. The real question is how the show is going to end. Who will eventually win the great spiritual war of the ages, Light or Darkness?

The choice always was and always will be yours. How will you respond?

How did the war get to this stage and this location Let's travel back in time....the flashback.

ORIGIN OF LUCIFER REBELLION
- THE FLASHBACK

"Spiritual warfare is very real. There's a furious, fierce, and ferocious battle raging in the realm of the spirit between the forces of God and the forces of evil. Warfare happens every day, all the time. Whether you believe it or not, you are on a battlefield. You are in warfare." — Pedro Okoro"

It is time to travel in time to the origins of Lucifer's actual rebellion itself. Records of this time are scattered and fragmentary–even in the Bible, the book of Urantia, or others, we may not have the full story and might never have it. Much of the history and physical evidence for what I am about to tell you has been intentionally destroyed by a side in the conflict. But countless hours of research, personal experiences, and a degree of "insider knowledge" have allowed me to give you the basics.

Just about every religion offers an account of the creation of the world. The Old Testament speaks of God separating the light and darkness and creating the heavens and the earth in seven days, and the Muslim holy text, the Quran, agrees with that account. All three of the Abrahamic faiths also speak of a great flood blotting out life on earth due to man's iniquity, and similar ideas can be seen in even polytheistic religions.

Plato, the Greek thinker who was arguably the father of the Western philosophical tradition in general, wrote in the Phaedo about how one's soul could be refined throughout lifetimes to eventually reach union with the Greek gods and how it never truly dies even though the body might. But there are Dark forces in addition to divine ones who are interested in our immortal souls. Some, as in the Abrahamic traditions, call him Lucifer, Satan, or Shaitan. The idea of a "Dark Lord" is prominent even in our entertainment and fantasy stories, like Sauron in The Lord of the Rings or Smith in The Matrix after he runs out of control. All of these are echoes of an important spiritual truth. This chapter will describe the leader of those Dark forces and what he has in store for us in reality.

GOD and Creation

God is the Deity. All things seen and unseen, known and unknown are created by Him. There is no beginning or ending to God, He is alpha and Omega. When God decided to experience Himself, He created Universe and filled it with life according to Bible. The purpose of all living things is to find a way back to their Creator, God. In this way God experiences His creation through the created.

God has created many different Angels, some Angels do not have free will and exist only for specific purposes. The Bible mentions that some angels are created to worship him and they encircle him with praise and song eternally.

Another group was created called Arch Angels and although smaller in number they had power and carried out God's wishes. They delivered messages, intervened in disputes or problems, and could decide to take an action that was directed or approved by God.

Lucifer

God Created Lucifer as a unique being in that he was an Angel, the most beautiful angel of all created, and he had free will, and the ability to make his own decisions and act on them. The original Aramaic name Lucifer translates to Morning Star. Lucifer is mentioned in the Bible only two times but is said to have sat at God's side and worshipped him and loved him deeply. Lucifer was regarded as the wisest, greatest, and most beautiful angel in all of creation. He is described as the most beautiful and brightest angel in existence and regarded as the perfection of beauty and wisdom. His beauty exceeded all other angels in heaven to the point where a mere glance would make anyone go mad from sheer beauty and power. He is noted to have six colossal whitish gold wings, that almost looked made of light. According to the Old Testament, when Lucifer was in heaven his clothing was adorned with many precious stones all beautifully crafted for him and set in the finest gold.

The War in Heaven

Lucifer was created as the best angel with great power and glory. Due to Lucifer being the favored creation, God would reveal to him, His plans for the creation. The more God told Lucifer His plans, the more problems Lucifer began to see. His thoughts began to stray from what his Father desired. Eventually, it led to a series of heated arguments between God and Lucifer. Lucifer started to question God and only grew infuriated by God's answers ending in God admonishing Lucifer each time.

Whenever Lucifer would leave, he would deduce that everything and everyone would be under the authority of God and all creatures eventually find their way back to God through one's experiences and that no one can go above God. Lucifer called this "predestination". Lucifer grew heavily opposed to this concept of "predestination"; which involves the destiny of all beings under God's will. Lucifer's pride began to overtake him and grew more rebellious against his Father. It soon led to Lucifer becoming dissatisfied with following God. Lucifer did not like to be under God's authority. He did not believe that anyone should be above him or be in control of him. Lucifer wanted to be like God and he wanted his own creation. He wanted complete autonomy and free will.

"I will ascent into heaven, I will exalt my throne above the starts of God; I will also sit on the mount of the congregation on the farthest sides of the north; I will also ascend the heights of the clouds, I will be like the Most High." – Isaiah 14:13-14

Lucifer's paranoia made him see God as a tyrannical ruler and declared that no one should control other lives and fate, instead, they should be free agents who have control over their choices and actions. He then proclaimed that he would rule in God's stead to rid the concept of predestination.

You (referring to Lucifer) were the anointed guardian cherub. I placed you; you were on the holy mountain of God; in the midst of the stones of fire you walked. – Ezekiel 28:14

Lucifer finally launched his "Declaration of Liberty". Lucifer declared before all the heavenly hosts, and legions of angels, that self-government should be the law of the universe and all should be freed from the Universal Father's 'yoke' and rule themselves. However, he also proclaimed that he was the "friend of men and angels" and "God of liberty".

He proposed a new Creation concept. Lucifer sincerely believed that with his new creation, he could enhance and fasten spiritual growth compared to the current process of step-by-step evolution under God's rule. Lucifer wanted to be the creator of souls, he thought that by using laboratory methods and his creative abilities, he is able to give a portion of his spirit to create new souls that can evolve faster with higher intelligence, that the current way under Gods ruling which is a slow, long and methodical process of evolution.

Additionally, Lucifer also proposed the concept of "karma", which is cause and effect. What you sow you reap. He sincerely believed that this will help the souls to learn and evolve faster. As talented and charming as he is, he was able to sell his concept of new creation and evolution to 1/3rd of the angels in heaven.

LUCIFER REBELLION - THE FALL FROM HEAVEN

And war broke out in Heaven: Michael and His angels fought with the dragon; and the dragon and his angels fought. – Revelations 12:7

With 1/3rd of the angels, Lucifer waged a full-fledged war against God. Lucifer has recruited his trump card "Satan" a high angel to be his second in command and Beelzebub as his lieutenant.

According to Lucifer, there will be no advancement if God is in control of every one's lives. God made the argument that He would only guide them and that they were free to choose their own paths. However, Lucifer was so intoxicated by his power and pride, that he chose not to listen.

A long, arduous, and terrible battle was fought between the two forces - God and Christ vs Lucifer and Satan. This battle is said to have ravaged all of Heaven. During the climax of the fight, Christ struck Lucifer with a savage blow making Lucifer back down briefly. Christ in a final attempt pleaded with Lucifer to stop this madness, but to no avail.

With God's help, Christ defeated and terribly wounded Lucifer and Satan.

God then banished Lucifer, Satan, and his followers from Heaven. And so did Lucifer Fall from grace with the utmost tragedy, horror, dismay, and terror.

He was cast to the Earth, and his angels were cast out with him. – Revelations 12:9

And I beheld Satan fall as lightning from heaven." - Luke 10:18

The Book of Isaiah also records this event –

"How you are fallen from heaven, O Lucifer, son of the morning! How you are cut down to the ground, you who weakened the nations! For you have said in your heart: 'I will ascend into heaven, I will exalt my throne above the stars of God; I will also sit on the mount of the congregation on the farthest sides of the north; I

will ascend above the heights of the clouds, I will be like the Most High'" (Isaiah 14:12-14).

Lucifer's Dominion over Hell

Despite the banishment from Heaven, the fallen angels were still allowed to roam the lower levels of Heaven and also the material world; their powers were limited. God, being as merciful as He is decided to give Lucifer a chance to prove that his philosophy and his creation is better. Lucifer was given dominion over a region in Christ's universe.

Despite his defeat, he retained his proud and fiercely defiant nature. He declared that the blow he and his brethren have received shall be returned to God by their own hands.

Satan

Before his fall from Heaven, Satan was more noble, just, and fair but strict and firm. He was an exalted cherub and thus had great pride over his power and position.

Satan is a powerful heavenly being, so much so that he was specifically chosen by Lucifer to be his ultimate trump card during the war in heaven. Next to both Christ and Lucifer, he is the most powerful angel created by God. After his fall from grace also, he wields immeasurable supernatural power although fairly weakened after being confined in Hell. However, Satan should not be underestimated as he remains the most powerful entity in all of Hell and Earth. He is praised for being the second most powerful being only next to Lucifer himself and rivaling Lucifer as well. He was strong enough to defeat an armada of angels and also challenge Christ. The immensity of his power is evident when he imbues his loyal followers with great demonic power allowing them to go head-to-head with other mighty angelic beings.

He is also known to be an accomplished master of black magic and has incredible knowledge in all manners of spells, having no superior other than possibly Lucifer. After he fell into the Abyss and emerged from the crater, he renounced his angelic name and went by the title of "Satan" which means Adversary. He emerged as a new being and one that would be against all that God had created. He chose the name "Satan" as a declaration that he will be the ultimate enemy of mankind.

Note: For the rest of the book the names Satan and Lucifer are used interchangeably.

FALL OF PLANET EARTH TO LUCIFER REBELLION

"Spiritual warfare is very real. There's a furious, fierce, and ferocious battle raging in the realm of the spirit between the forces of God and the forces of evil. Warfare happens every day, all the time. Whether you believe it or not, you are on a battlefield. You are in warfare." — Pedro Okoro

In the grand constellation picture, planet Earth is one of the unique shining "Pearl" created by Christ with the help of God. The illumination of the crystal blueish color is extremely eye-catching and glittering among the shining stars in the local universe. Earth attracted many space travelers to check out and set foot on the surface. Some of them were involved to set up their settlements when their "Home" planets were in "trouble". All their needs and wants were fully met and supplied without conditions. Their descendants were living without worry and with full compassion and love, walking freely with abundance while learning their lessons and experiences. All lived a high nobility life and worked toward their soul evolutionary journey.

Lucifer/Satan and his cohorts gradually expanded their control beyond their designated region of the universe. About 200,000 years ago the rebellion entered our section of the galaxy and then Earth. Many leaders of the different planets were either captured or taken over cleverly by Satan. Leaders and planetary princes (a planetary prince can be likened to the president/prime minister of the planet) of more than 700 planets bowed to Lucifer.

Lucifer is unanimously elected as the head of the region of which our planet Earth is part. This region consists of numerous inhabited worlds. Soon this region of the universe became infested with darkness. Some of the lighted creations were also affected. Darkness is very real and intelligent. We will see later why this is so. The spiritual armies of Light and Dark would eventually clash directly.

God and Christ saw that things were not going well for the Universe and decided to localize the battle. This served two purposes. First to attract all darkness to the identified world(s), so the effects can be localized and the dark army's fate can be determined once and for all; secondly, the localization can prevent further dark infestation to other sections of the universe.

The planetary prince of Earth at that time is Caligastia according to Urantia book. Lucifer successfully swayed Caligastia to join his rebellion. They established headquarters in Mesopotamia. This is the beginning of the fall of Earth. Lucifer and Satan successfully breached the barrier between Hell and Earth, this signaled the beginning of the Apocalypse.

I call the trio of Lucifer, Satan, and Caligastia as the real axis of evil.

Dark leaders were given some incentives in order to localize the battle, and they took the bait. Soon the darkness came to be localized to one single planet Earth. The fate of the dark and the fate of the universe will be decided on this little planet.

In Cosmos, planet Earth came to be known as a 'Prison Planet' or a 'Planet of Sorrows'.

MATRIX created on Planet Earth

"God is up to something or the dark armies would not be fighting this hard." – Trinity Royal

The Lucifer rebellion produced many changes on Earth. Darkness began to spread rapidly on Earth as the rebellion is centered on this planet. This caused much concern for God, Christ, and lighted beings.

According to the Truth book and Urantia, the supervisor authority from Lighted realms overseeing the spiritual development of planet Earth is Andovontia. He along with Christ made a decision to isolate Earth from the rest of the universe, and then hope to find a way to restore balance.

Isolation of Earth – The communication channels to and from Earth were shut-down. The interplanetary communication circuits were closed. The communication circuits between Earth Universe were shut down. This made it hard for celestial beings to communicate with earthlings.

The result is that Earth is isolated and spiritually quarantined. Earth is locked down.

Briefly stated the spiritual matrix is a great veil that was put in place on Earth to confine its inhabitants and sequester them away from the rest of the universe. This was done for the good of the entire universe, so the darkness contained in this region of space could not spread.

This spiritual isolation is what I call "The Real Matrix".

How Do You Know You Are Inside the Matrix?

It can be easier to understand by describing what the matrix, the veil around our world, is not. It isn't something you can just see, touch, taste, smell, or hear. It is, rather, a state of mind and being. You know you are not in the spiritual matrix if you and your fellow human beings are living fulfilled lives full of love, feeling no pain, with all of your material and emotional needs met. No one is trying to control you, all life, human and animal alike, is honored as part of a great unit (that is to say, you are living in harmony with nature), and nothing is separating you from the rest of creation. You will be able to get direct knowledge from your well-wishers from higher realms.

The lifespan of you and your friends is measured in centuries, you can communicate easily with angels, spirits, and other higher beings, you are attuned to your spiritual senses in addition to your five physical ones, and, in general, your life is not only long, satisfying, and purposeful, but also self-actualized: You do valuable work in your community which not only helps others but brings satisfaction to you, allowing you to grow and increase your talents. You are not struggling to provide food, clothes, and, shelter; rather you are flourishing in every way your soul desires. Your soul learns its lessons and progresses on its spiritual journey and is not quarantined or inhibited in any way.

This surely doesn't sound like the world most of us live in; this is because most of us are trapped in the spiritual matrix, albeit to different extents. This matrix cuts us off from true reality, making it harder to reach spiritual truths and higher beings. Most of us struggle to make it through our lives, and it seems like only a few powerful and influential people control everything, with the rest of us treated like sheep. Sometimes it seems like you, me, and our fellow human beings are just cattle being sacrificed by the rulers for their purposes—as if we were all entirely disposable rather than having our own valuable souls.

This is because, as Morpheus from the movie might say, the **Matrix has you**. You are suffering from mind control, working towards the ends of the Dark forces even though you don't consciously want to. All the inconveniences and injustices in your life are there to distract your mind and keep you from focusing on higher spiritual realities, which would help you break free from the matrix if you could concentrate on them. This unconscious programming affects not only you—it's not your fault for falling for it. All of humanity's collective psyche is also a victim of this scheme. Unconsciously, most people support the agenda of darkness, but there are and have always been certain individuals who break free of it to lead you and others away from the darkness.

Jesus Christ was one and the most important and famous, of course, but there have been many others as well. You can learn this by studying history and opening yourself to the wisdom of many great teachers.

Dark Philosophy

But by looking at history since then and analyzing the effects of Luciferian philosophy on our world today, we can make some very educated guesses. The heart of Lucifer's philosophy is egoism—or service to self. When he was still on God's side, Lucifer thought about fulfilling God's orders and maintaining a good, reasonable place in a larger order beyond himself. He thought about his fellow messengers and how to do right by all the lesser creatures God had set him to oversee.

Lucifer began thinking less and less of others and more and more about himself. He grew blinded by his own talent and skill, impressive as it might have been, and forgot that he relied on God and others to reach his full potential. Thus, he began to care about personal pride, and self-aggrandizement more than anything else.

He was not happy with how God runs the creation; he felt the system needed to be more boxy or have more controls. It needed more rules. He felt with his ideas, he could actually speed up evolution. In his quest to do his own thing, he created a very limiting box, thereby creating the very thing he did not want.

And for Lucifer and his Dark forces, ascension is all or nothing. Rather than allowing free individuals to ascend to Heavens or higher realms, as is appropriate for them, Lucifer believed that everyone should ascend or no one at all could ascend. He did not allow normal soul progression as seen in on evolving inhabited worlds. He established certain processes by means of which he converted Earth into a prison planet. Souls were not allowed to move out on their journey to Heaven after death sleep as God desired for his creation. Graduation of souls to Heaven has become a problem.

Concept of Karma as introduced by Lucifer

It was Lucifer that created the "karma" system we currently have on the planet, and that is not exactly natural either. Karma is for the purpose of learning cause and effect. Lucifer thought he could speed evolution by having each person experience the opposite in a lifetime or future lifetime of any experience, both sides of the coin so to speak.

And in doing so, he created a system that perpetuates the maladaptive behavior on the Earth plane. A simple example of this: If a person commits murder or several, then that person is supposed to be murdered an equal number of times, and that requires more murderers. if a person is raped, that person becomes a rapist.

He created the perfect system to keep this planet in an antichrist status, and it was rotten to the core. He destroyed free will; the very free will he proposed should exist for himself and others. He had abundant help in creating all of that, from others who chose to partake in his project.

We shall see in later chapters, how Christ's bestowal incarnation on this little planet Earth changed the concept of Karma as it no longer has the same teeth. The concept of an eye for an eye has been removed in the first coming of Christ.

God's Philosophy

By contrast, the philosophy of Light—God's plans for the universe— emphasizes both individual freedom and the importance of working to make things better for everyone. These two goals do not conflict but are in harmony. The first and most important is free will. God created companions to share his love with, not mindless automatons. He does not want to make people slaves as Lucifer does. He wants all of his creatures, on earth and elsewhere, to know and love him out of their own free will, a choice they make by using their minds and their spiritual senses to come to the correct conclusions on their own.

As a result of this freedom, God allows anyone to ascend at any time when they are ready, and there are always second chances for those who fail but want to get better. God respects how every individual can take a longer or shorter path through enlightenment, giving guidance as needed. However, they are always rising rather than being chained down as Lucifer would want.

It is important to note, that God does not demand any specific acts of worship or ritual. He does not bend or coerce or compel the free will of spiritual and sentient beings—allowing them to seek him or reject him under their power.

This brings us to the final part of Light's philosophy: altruism or Service to Others. Just as God cares for his creations, his creations should care for each other and sacrifice their short-term interests in the name of love and peace to benefit other people. Someone following the path of Light will be less concerned with their own power and prestige and more concerned with the happiness of their loved ones and humanity (as they ascend, all of creation) as a whole. They will carry out actions like donating to charity, volunteering their time, treating everyone with respect, and being honest in all of their dealings so that the entire community will benefit, even if it means they might not make as much money or fame directly.

PURPOSE OF THE WAR - FOR YOUR SOUL

"The enemy is fighting you because you have a purpose, a destiny with God as your provider."
- Trinity Royal

Now that the Earth is under the control and influence of Dark Lords - Lucifer, Satan, and Caligastia; it has become a challenge for Humanity to grow spiritually and become closer to God. So God sent many beings over many centuries to advance the cause of Light. But what exactly do these beings of Light teach? All great teachers taught us how to grow in consciousness and become closer to God.

It is your soul that both Darkness and Light are after. Both Light and Dark are fighting for control of your soul, the planet, and the humans on it. This single planet can change the course of the entire war for either side. We will discuss this more in the coming sections.

How the War is Fought

You're surely familiar with warfare from just watching the news. Whether it's the conflict in Ukraine as of the time of this writing, the Gulf War back in the 1990s, or the Vietnam War even earlier, you're probably familiar with the sound of gunfire, explosions, cannons, and missiles from jet planes flying overhead. But even those wars, as brutal as they were, had some rules attached to them. For instance, even though American and Soviet-backed countries fought constantly during the Cold War, neither the US nor the USSR used nuclear weapons against each other directly. The spiritual conflict between Light and Dark is a total war in the truest sense, occurring over thousands of years and on many different planes of existence. But it, too, has rules, and you must be aware of those rules to make the right choices during the conflict.

The first rule is non-interference, at least directly. Satan and his angels will not physically manifest on earth and do battle with weapons like swords and guns, and neither will the forces of Light. Combat, for now, is mostly in unseen spiritual realms, as both sides try to gain influence over particular human beings who can shape human society as a whole in ways more amenable to one side or another. However, humans can petition either side for certain types of help if they ask directly. We will cover these sorts of rituals in a future chapter, but for now, just keep in mind that by contacting Satan's agents, humans can use the power of darkness to gain the knowledge they might not otherwise have had or use spells to cloud people's mind or gain social or political influence. Contacting beings of Light can offer more positive effects, both personally—providing better mental health and a sense of well-being—and on a larger scale, by soothing people's minds to make them more peaceful or appealing to their better natures to give rise to positive social programs or matters like that.

By the same token, the veil—or the spiritual matrix—cannot be removed. The vast majority of human beings on earth are unaware of this spiritual conflict. And even those who are aware of it, like you are now, cannot see everything going on in the great Light-Dark war. While you may be able to recollect some wisdom from them under very particular circumstances, and while the virtue you display in this life has some impact, you lose virtually all of your concrete memories when you pass away. That is precisely why you should try to do the best you can in this one. You must rely on yourself to navigate the time you spend on earth that you're aware of. You can't rely on past glories (if you had any) to carry you. The wisdom contained in this book can help you make up for past mistakes you might have committed and set you back on the path to advancement. The Universal Father's mercy is boundless, and he wants everyone to reach Him eventually, no matter how long it takes or how much difficulty they might have.

DNA

The one exception to these rules can be found in our DNA. Living in the modern world, you're probably aware of how DNA is the building block of life, the blueprint according to which our cells grow and develop, and thus the foundation of our physical bodies. However, DNA contains traces of spiritual truth as well. With special training, you can access buried memories within your DNA. It can be very hard to get full memories, so most of the time, you can only access fragments, but once you know of the existence of the spiritual matrix, and higher levels of existence (heavens), your soul journey can be enlightening.

Some of these memories in your DNA contain 'codes' for not only moral virtue and heroism in the universe, but the secrets of enlightenment and advancement towards higher levels of consciousness. This knowledge is supernatural in the truest sense—even if you had not experienced it so far, the Universal Father and his angels spread it throughout the fabric of the universe, where it became attached to certain strands of DNA. This supernatural genetic knowledge is crucial to future battles in the great war; the next chapter of this book will describe its role in more depth. You, as an individual, can influence how the entire universe will turn out!

The Prize: Your Soul

In The Matrix, Morpheus tells Neo about the war between humans and machines in the early 22nd century and how the machines won but did not destroy humanity entirely. When humans created autonomous machines, they were powered by solar energy, so when the war started, humans used nanomachines to blot out the sky.

The machines, however, found a new power source—the bioelectric and thermal energies of the human body. Thus, with overwhelming numbers, the machines crushed the human militaries and attached the survivors to gigantic power plants, where their bodies would be used to power the machine civilization. This would be hard to do if the humans remained conscious, so the machines created a false reality, the Matrix and performed surgery on the humans (drilling holes in their skulls and creating mechanical interfaces between organic brains and machine computers), and ensconced all of them inside that false virtual reality.

Satan's goal is not quite the same. Being spiritual rather than material creatures, the forces of Darkness do not need the "bioelectrical and thermal" energies of the human body. However, the Matrix described by Morpheus in the movie can be a useful way of thinking about the spiritual matrix that exists in reality. Satan does not want our bodies in and of themselves, but our minds–our souls–generate energy that his forces desperately need. The darkness feeds off negative emotional energies from humans. This makes Dark beings strong. The stronger they are, the more darkness they hold. Higher Dark entities can effortlessly subjugate a normal human being. Once you are subjugated and controlled, you become a weapon of Darkness. You are mind-controlled.

Souls are eternal and pass through time by gaining different experiences. Death of the human physical body is not the end for ensouled beings that can think. Now, the activity of the soul—that which directs us towards good, virtuous deeds (producing illuminated, holy souls) or evil ones (producing tainted, condemned souls)—

creates spiritual echoes across the universe, including the heavenly realms from which Satan originally came, reaching all the way to Paradise. However, the actions of souls, mediated through the physical shells they currently occupy, can be good or bad. This energy is used by either side to further the agenda.

Many creatures from all across the universe can provide spiritual energy in this way. But humans on earth, due to the intensity with which we live our lives and the strength of the beliefs we hold, consequently have strong, bright souls, which generate immense amounts of this energy. Therein lies the heart of Satan's plan. For reasons we will discuss in future chapters, he and his army cannot physically manifest on earth en-masse at this time. If they could, they would just subjugate all of us, and that would be that. However, by gaining control of the world through manipulating its dark-hearted leaders (the 'princes' of our planet, to use Biblical phrasing), Satan plans to turn it into a gigantic prison of shadows. There, human beings will be enslaved and trapped, our souls no longer able to advance to higher realms in Heaven. Our souls will be imprisoned on earth, where they will be used to fuel Satan and his fallen angels in their dark crusade against the Universal Father and his loyal ones. You can see why I mentioned The Matrix. Just like the machines needed human bodies and thus could not simply destroy our species, Satan needs human souls and cannot just annihilate us. And just like the machines used a virtual reality Matrix to entrap human minds, Satan wants to do something similar with human souls.

Light, by contrast, does not want to trap souls for selfish use—quite the opposite. The forces of Light want Earth and its human populations to evolve rather than stagnate and languish in prison. When human beings express virtue and thus ascend to higher levels of consciousness or higher vibratory levels (to use technical terms), their souls emit light energy which strengthens God's forces to help free more souls from this Matrix. This is good for both individuals and the universe as a whole, and the souls who, over many lifetimes, have ascended to the highest vibratory level of all (Paradise) are true juggernauts in the struggle against darkness.

Thus, both sides have a very vested interest in you. Yes, you, the person reading this book right now! Your actions here and now, in this world, and the beliefs you hold, not only influence your life but the lives you will live, by extension, the color of your soul. This will ultimately influence the course of the final battle between Light and Dark–which side will your soul's energy go to? You must make the right decision. In the majority of the cases, the choices have already been made. Ample time has been given, extended grace periods have been given, and much knowledge has been shared with Humanity. Whether you go to light or darkness has to do with the gravitational pull of your soul in this time on Earth which is changeable —more on this subject in future chapters.

Birth and Evolution of the Soul

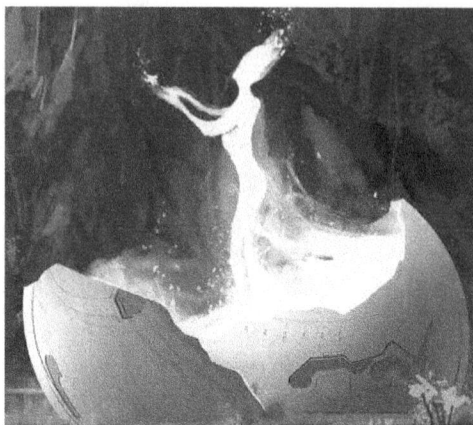

To truly understand the spiritual struggle, you need to understand its relationship with the material world. To quickly review, let us go over the several parts of a full human being.

First is your physical body–what Morpheus in The Matrix movie referred to with his quote about bioelectric and thermal energy. This is what breathes, grows, gets healthy or sick, is made out of cells like all other creatures, and so on.

Then is the mind. This is most closely associated with the brain of the physical body, and this is what thinkers refer to when they talk about what interprets sense experience, what has emotions, what makes judgments, and so on. This is the physical aspect of what sets human beings and other sentient creatures above animals and plants. Mind is the seat of the soul. This is something acquired and tuned through experience. The soul is what the human spirit becomes through experience, whether choosing to conform to the Divine Will or reject it. In any case, this is the immortal part of a human being that survives his or her death.

The third is the spirit, which is divine. This aspect of a human being actually precedes his or her personality and becomes part of a person when they are born and start interacting with the world. It is called by many names including "small voice with-in", "Father with-in", "Thought Adjuster", "Higher self" etc. This is God's gift to each of us. This is God's Spirit residing in us and helps attune human beings to the Divine Will.

A short expert from one of my books "**From Suffering to Healing**"

The soul is constantly bathed in the influx of energies in the universe. What you choose to do with the energy determines your soul's experiences. Some of your experiences contribute to your soul's growth and development, while other experiences might not. The soul is meant to experience a multitude of trials and tribulations along its journey. You might wonder where your soul is journeying to, and the answer is that your soul is on a quest to enrich itself and then return to its source of origin in the universe. The universe is structured to assist your soul in making choices. In a way, the universe is in a conspiracy for your soul's growth as it is in the world's favor for you to grow fully into your soul's potential. During this journey, your soul has acquired and will continue to acquire "various experiences, both good and bad, favorable and unfavorable, positive and negative. However, to continue its journey back to the source of its creation, all of the residual bad, unfavorable, negative energy has to be discarded. When you shed that negative residue, your energetic vibration will be high enough for your soul to endure the frequencies of the higher realms.

CLARION CALL FROM GOD TO ALL THE ANGELS IN HEAVEN

What takes place on Earth is very important to Heaven. - Trinity Royal

I n the previous chapters, you've learned about the spiritual forces at play throughout history and in the world right now. Even though they are unknown to the vast majority of humanity, you have chosen to open your eyes and discover how they have been and are influencing you and everyone around you. As Morpheus would say, You have taken the red pill.

With the knowledge you now possess, it is time to move on to more advanced topics where you will gain significantly more depth of knowledge. While you've learned about the spiritual Matrix, and how Dark-aligned and Light-aligned entities influence Earth-whether by enslaving humans or liberating them, encouraging selfishness rather than altruism, and so on, now you'll see specific instances of these activities-and the rationales behind specific plans launched by both sides in the war- especially centering around Jesus Christ and His teachings.

Why God Needs Your Help

We have seen in the previous chapters that the War came to be centered on planet Earth. Earth is the epicenter of the battle between Dark and Light. What happens here affects the rest of the Universe.

Due to this, the human race has become God's prized possession, and our planet Earth- also called Urantia in higher realms of consciousness-is the site of many of God's most important plans and a storehouse of His most valuable resources. For the purposes of this book, we don't need to go too far into the details of the Universal Father's creative activity, or every one of His agents. Here, we will simply go over the broadest, most basic points of Earth's history you need to know to get a grasp of what you need to do to help the forces of Light.

God's own son "the Son of God" is Christ, who is also the creator of the Universe. Millions of years ago, Christ manipulated many nebulae to form stars, and thus our galaxy, and around one of these stars at the edge of one of these galaxies is the Milky Way. Each galaxy consists of numerous solar systems and planets.

When our Creator created this planet, He noted that there was something special about this little blue orb, it became known as the "seed" planet. The seed planets are considered special as new souls are developed on these kinds of planets. The seed planets are the training ground for young Souls on an evolutionary path. There are very few in number in this part of our galaxy. Christ with the help of Trinity consciousness (God the Universal Father, Eternal, Son, and Infinite Spirit) created the Human species. So we are created in His "likeness" as the scriptures state, making the residents of our planet particularly important for the plans of both God and Satan.

Human beings evolved empathy, compassion, altruism, and especially religious feelings much earlier in our development than was the case for sentient beings in other worlds. As a result, the spiritual energies produced by the development of human souls, whether ascending towards higher consciousness realms as the Light desires or chained down to this lower dimensional consciousness as the Dark desires, far outweigh those produced by even heavenly beings in the universe. Since the war has been at a stalemate in the rest of the Universe for a very long time, with neither Lucifer's forces nor the Light has been able to dislodge the other, Earth has taken center stage as the decisive point. Darkness, unfortunately, has managed to make significant in-roads on our planet and has advanced its plans very far. On the other hand, the Universal Father has plans of his own involving His most powerful agent here: Jesus Christ, whom we shall learn more about in future chapters. This should suffice as an overview of the Universal Father treasures humanity in particular so much.

Effects of the Rebellion

Now, due to Lucifer's rebellion, discussed in previous chapters, God has had a very difficult time reaching out to humanity, protecting and guiding us, despite how highly He valued us. The path for growth toward the Light was growing harder and harder for us, with many obstacles placed in our way. Here are some of the ways Darkness has interfered with us:

- No real religious teachings. There have been many great religions started by enlightened prophets which have been stamped out by the Dark. Humanity has been made to forget these religions and their teachings to delay the growth of many strong souls and prevent knowledge about the great spiritual conflict from spreading widely.

- Manipulation of teachings. Cunning agents of Darkness have manipulated some teachings of religions throughout history–and in the present day–to sow confusion and make it even harder for seekers to attain genuine knowledge of Heaven and higher spiritual realms.

- Over-emphasis on the process: Partially due to machinations from the Dark, but also due to honest mistakes which built up over time, much of humanity has become too focused on ritual–rather than finding their own individual "spark" of God within themselves.

Finally, whereas direct communication with God is possible on higher realms that are more vibrationally attuned to

Paradise–the Veil or Matrix which envelopes Earth has cut us off from the Divine in some way. Only if we are very fortunate can some of us access higher realities, and often only in dreams; communion with the Universal Father Himself is very rare, with only the Bestowal of Christ giving us hope (described in the next chapter).

Even so, there are some agents of the Light who have come to Earth to assist us in reaching higher consciousness levels, even if they were not in direct contact with the Divine. Some gods in ancient polytheistic or henotheistic religions were heavenly messengers who came to help Humanity in the evolution process. Also religious figures like Lord Buddha or Lord Krishna, philosophers like Aristotle, Plato, Zeno of Elea, Confucius, and some modern-day personages like Martin Luther King. Some angels even gave inspiration to great inventors and teachers, like Jonas Salk–creator of the polio vaccine, Albert Einstein, and other Nobel Prize winners.

All these people were sent or influenced by the Light to guide mankind towards the climactic event which will occur soon, in the present time we are living in. The Dark has also influenced our world in many ways, both enslaving individual humans, trapping their souls, encouraging the evolution of dark cults, and, teaching other individuals selfish methods of increasing their power and influence. Some Dark agents manifested in this world directly, putting on human disguises, while others merely contacted ordinary people seeking power and subtly guided them into the shadows. Many Dark agents or servants settled as kings, queens, or great and bloody conquerors. Adolf Hitler and Ghenghis Khan are two such examples. Less famously, Dark agents generally tried–and are still trying–to infiltrate large, powerful, centralized governments to control information and how people lived, to ensure as few as possible could ascend. They also manipulate the genetic code of humanity, to cut out strands of DNA carrying Light codes–such as nobler, more altruistic temperaments, higher attunement to spiritual realities, a higher propensity to dream–and so on.

Despite both sides doing their best throughout hundreds of thousands of years, Light was never able to break Dark's grasp on the world, and Dark could never remove every trace of Light from Earth, even as its influence steadily grew. Thus, the war on Earth was grinding down into a stalemate as well; whatever advantages Dark had would take many, many centuries to come to fruition. Before that can happen, the forces of Light desire to strike a shattering blow against Satan/Lucifer. The fallen Morning Star, cunning as he is, anticipated that, and is attempting to gather his forces for his decisive annihilation of Light on Earth, which will allow him to capture the planet and turn all of the prodigious energy humans produce into his ends.

God's Counterattack

As the situation on Earth is rapidly heating up, the Universal Father focused more and more of His energies and attention on it. About 200,000 years ago, He made a clarion call to all of His angels to focus on humanity and do all they can to uplift the consciousness of this blue orb. God is no fool and made clear to His angelic forces that this would likely be the most difficult mission they had ever attempted ever in their entire existence. God also emphasized to them this struggle was worth it, for He realized how unique and powerful humanity is due to its peculiar evolutionary history, and thus He loves humanity and Earth more than any other place in the Universe. Much of God's focus is on humanity and earth at the present time. This is an absolute fact.

This clarion call rang out wide to all of Heavens and Paradise. The mission was simply to save Humans and Earth. A mission like this was never attempted in the history of creation.

Since this was unique, a vast number of angels had no idea what to expect and did not sign up for the mission. Given the incredible skills, the angels possessed, very many of them could not take it for fear of the unknown. Many were afraid of the struggle and Satan's forces in general and were also uncertain of the outcome. Most have already witnessed the devastation caused by Lucifer's rebellion in the Heavens. After all, such an endeavor had never been attempted before, and no histories existed in the great archives and annals of Heaven that could give any guidance on a war like this. The angels who raised these concerns did not have full faith in the Universal Father's victory, so they chose to sit out the battle and wait and see who would win. Others did not want to limit their consciousness by focusing on one planet in one system in one planet of the vast Universe.

In fairness to these seemingly cowardly angels, fighting Satan's forces on Earth is a truly monumental task. The Matrix surrounding Earth has several characteristics that make things harder for the Light than the Dark.

However, some angels did have faith in God and Christ and said "yes" to this divine mission. There were at least 144,000 of these according to the Holy Bible. These are the angles who have agreed to come into the Matrix and be part of the Matrix, mingle with evolving Human souls, and increase the vibrations of Human consciousness thereby helping God and the cause of light. These angels were known as descended angels. According to a divinely orchestrated plan, these brave angelic souls planted themselves at predetermined strategic points of Human evolution to become teachers, preachers, inventors, gurus, sadhus, scientists..etc. Basically to teach and help evolve Humanity.

> Then I looked, and behold, the Lamb was standing on Mount Zion, and with Him one hundred and forty-four thousand, having His name and the name of His Father written on their foreheads. – Revelations 14:1

However life is not all rosy for these brave angels; by being in the Matrix, all of them got caught up in the illusion of the Matrix, and most if not all forgot their divine origins and inter-mingled with humans over the period of 200,000 years. This has helped to manipulate the DNA of the Human species, thereby evolving the human species faster and closer to God. If Light wins, these brave angels will enjoy all the splendor and accolades they have earned.

The Matrix prevents spiritual beings from heavenly realms from passing into Earth. They are only allowed in if a resident of Earth, within the Matrix itself, specifically asks them to enter. This is called the doctrine of non-interference. Some beings can get around this, but it is extremely rare, and Dark forces like demons and shadow-whisperers more often do this. The great Bestowal of Christ was one exception to this rule in Light's favor. Another exception was the case of 'original seeders,' angels who visited humanity in distant past eons to place Light information in our genomes.

The effects of the Matrix on the development of the soul itself present another obstacle to the cause of Light due to loss of memory. Souls, ignorant as they are, cannot easily coordinate with each other, or angelic beings, and must rely on their internal abilities to evolve, which can be made easier if the bodies to which they are reincarnated possess useful strands of Light-aligned DNA. In this regard, humans possessing these types of DNA should mingle as much as possible with the rest of the human population to spread them far and wide and to future generations, but again, since accumulated knowledge is lost, this is harder to do. Souls must also learn their own lessons, rather than being taught, how to avoid the pitfalls of the Dark, transform Dark energies into Light ones, and enhance the collective consciousness of humanity.

Given all this, you can imagine why God is personally concerned with this war on a single small planet and refuses to give up on the human race. It is extremely important for Him and the Light to win this war, as so many of His strongest angels have already invested so much. In other words, not only are human souls at stake, but Paradise and other types of angels from higher heavenly realms also have vulnerable souls that might be at risk if they lose. Thus, God has a vested interest in you—yes, you! He wants your soul to grow, advance, and improve your spiritual life so you can help in the struggle. This will determine whether Light or Dark wins in the end.

MATRIX EXPLAINED - AGENDA OF LIGHT AND DARK

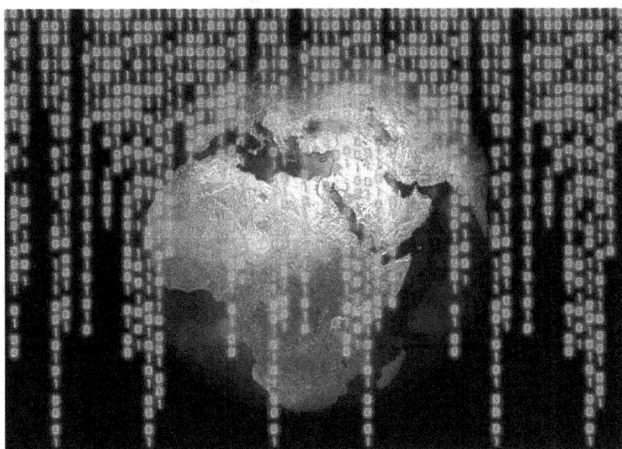

"Spiritual Warfare is the unseen battle God wages on your behalf." -Jim George

Rules of Matrix

Ever since Lucifer's rebellion entered this sector of the galaxy 200,000 years ago, Satan and his Dark forces have plotted to turn all the physical worlds over to his dark plans. Since, as described, Dark and Light forces cannot physically manifest to attack each other as normal armies would, their struggle is spiritual—in one sense—but also social, political, and diplomatic in another sense. Both sides need to influence the native residents of the planet (the material creatures that live in them as opposed to angelic beings of Heaven). The forces of Light and Dark do this so that the entire societies become more favorable to one side or another, and thus dedicated to generating spiritual energy for either side. Towards this end, both Dark and Light beings have descended into various material planes of existence. Following the doctrine of non-interference, but has to abide by the rules of the Matrix.

Loss of Memory - These souls will take birth as human babies and grow in the Matrix. Once the soul enters the Matrix, the soul will have no conscious memories, meaning the slate is clean. Depending on the soul's makeup and the gravitational pull of past experiences stored in the subconscious, the ensouled being will either want to control and contribute to dark deeds or educate and enlighten people to higher truths.

In a generalized sense, dark beings gravitate toward positions of power and influence; light beings gravitate towards teachers, helpers, and service-oriented. A general 80-20 rule applies. There are always exceptions. So this should not be taken literally as is.

Also, it is important to note that sometimes Light purposefully serves darkness to learn the ways of the dark and also to bring more experience to themselves and collective light consciousness. So I would not judge anyone. Everyone is part of a puzzle piece. We may never know the higher reasons for each soul at any given time in any location or society.

Most of the time, emissaries of the Dark pose as people of great power— prime ministers, presidents, kings, queens, generals, and so on. In modern society, they might also be the CEOs of large companies, big media personalities, 'influencers,' and so on. Any social or political position that allows one to control masses of people and especially dominate their thinking or circumscribe their freedom is an attractive one for Satan and his minions.

Servants of Light, on the other hand, are more likely to become teachers, inventors, scientists, doctors, philosophers, yogis, or gurus. Generally, any position in which one can encourage others to find enlightenment and ascension, preach moral virtues and altruism, and put into action positive modes of thought will be more attractive to the Light. Jesus Christ, of course, is the most obvious example of this sort of influence, but there have been many others before and since.

How Representatives of Dark Influence the World

The above descriptions are general guidelines, not absolute rules— there have been scientists, teachers, and gurus who spread teachings of darkness, and politicians and monarchs who have spread the Light. A more reliable guide for telling them apart revolves around the specific actions such leaders may take and the goals they work towards. Also, keep in mind that it can be very difficult to tell if an individual is an agent of either side in disguise or simply in contact with such a spiritual agent, or indirectly controlled by one.

Representatives of darkness will invariably follow Satan's teachings in the end, as described in chapter one; egoism (service to self), boxing people in, growing at the cost of others, turning people into mere sheep to be exploited, and so on. This section highlights some of these tactics used by dark forces. I am purposefully keeping this short to not cross the fine line of truth vs conspiracy theories.

- **Boxing people and removing freedom:** Servants of the Dark will try to pass laws or enact social policies that reduce individual freedom and make it harder for people to break free of a system. While total freedom might lead to anarchy, Dark ones try to reduce freedom in ways that do not lead to greater safety or prosperity for society. Restrictions on free speech, religion, or travel, laws upholding racial discrimination, and so on, are the sorts of things Dark leaders favor.

- **Growing at the cost of others:** Dark societies are usually organized around the lines of social Darwinism. Rather than the individuals who make up a community helping each other with their problems, Dark leaders will encourage them to make money or cultivate influence by keeping others down and stabbing each other in the back, ostensibly so only the 'strongest' will rise to the top while the 'weaker' perish. This is the essence of Satan's egoistic "Service to Self" ideals; only working for oneself without regard for anyone else, even if you have to hurt others to get ahead.

- **Control of information and all outlets of knowledge:** To keep knowledge of Light and its teachings from spreading, Dark leaders will suppress or try to gain absolute control of all forms of media (like newspapers, online news sites, and so on) as well as all education institutions (not just colleges and universities, but even schools for young children and teenagers) so that the truth is only on the surface. Our idiot boxes (aka TV) is a highly controlled aspect, repeating the dark philosophy sugar-coated with truths over and over again with different names and different faces.

- **Use of technology:** This is a huge topic, very briefly stated here. Humanity is in the lower rungs of consciousness so our perception of life and the universe is very limited. There are technologies by both Dark and Light that are beyond current human understanding. The beings have been in existence for millions of years compared to a few hundred years of technological advancement of the human species. AI is just one of the technology that Humans are exploring currently.

- **Cultivating a sheep mentality for humans**: Related to this, Dark leaders will try to prevent independent thought among those they control and train their societies to follow the commands of politicians or monarchs without thinking. We are like sheep being pulled to the slaughterhouse. (The great light beings of the cosmos watch with great sadness as the humans are being taken to the slaughterhouse of their own volition).

- **Distortion of religious scriptures and teachings:** Ensouled Humans are wired such that there is an upward gravitational pull to grow, evolve, and become closer to heaven and the source. Religion is a natural element that aids in growth. Dark beings use this as a powerful weapon. Most organized religions of today are controlled in so many ways. It is beyond the scope to discuss anything more on this.

- **Creating more Karma:** To be discussed in future chapters, Dark entities want people to generate negative, rather than positive, karma to keep their souls trapped in this universe, so their spiritual activity creates energy for Satan's side. Thus, they will allow humans to survive but not truly flourish.

- **DNA manipulation:** Dark politicians and scientists try to find out fragments of DNA in people that can confer enlightenment and destroy them. They have also tried to manipulate DNA in people (often without their consent) to make their servants more malleable and dull-witted. Over time, they want to alter human evolution to create as many subservient slaves as possible and have done this throughout history and continue to do so in sophisticated ways. Many people barely notice it; it is as subtle and omnipresent as the Matrix in that Morpheus and Neo fought. There are many books and movies that capture the importance of DNA for evolution. There is some level of truth in these books and or movies.

- **Suppressing Knowledge:** This is the most important aspect of Dark plans. They want to suppress knowledge of all higher spiritual realities and destroy all evidence of humanity's past to better control us.

- **Influential organizations:** Dark ones will create groups such as the Illuminati, subversive cults, and certain Freemason groups (though not all!) to carry out their plans. Some groups will openly declare that they support Satan's rebellion, like the "Children of Satan" or "Fallen Angels," and so on. Sometimes Dark entities in disguise will lead these organizations, while other times they are led by mere humans who are in contact with Dark entities. These groups will try to make themselves out to be harmless or even sometimes philanthropic—but they will always be dedicated, in reality, to getting their adherents into positions of power. They will try to cultivate politicians and make their own members CEOs, tech moguls, and so on. This is one way Satan tries to win the conflict while still obeying the rules of non-interference.

- **Keeping power/positions within families**: Enough said, you get the picture.

- **Deceit**: This is probably the most powerful weapon of Darkness in my opinion. Do you recollect any events in recent history that has taken away your liberties and freedom in the name of so-called security? Every liberty taken away from the people is a gain for the Dark agenda. Dark is very very intelligent in how it operates. Conditions are created so that Humans willingly give away liberties and freedom. It is beyond the scope to go any further. This is your homework. Can you think of any events or situations in the world that made you give your freedom away little by little?

- **Selling souls to the devil:** This is the last way Satan tries to carry out his agenda. To make the Dark more attractive, sometimes Satan's fallen angel servants, or other supernatural Dark entities, attach themselves to ordinary people to make them much more knowledgeable and influential in certain affairs than they would otherwise be. Someone with only modest speaking ability might become a great and convincing orator overnight, for instance. Someone with mediocre academic accomplishments might suddenly seem to become vastly more intelligent and immediately become a skilled doctor, technician, engineer, or scientist. Or someone might suddenly gain mysterious knowledge about the stock market or other economic matters and use it to become very, very rich in a matter of days. In every case, they will become more influential in politics or society and thus more able to increase the influence of Darkness over the world as a whole. Sometimes this is random, but other times desperate or immoral people can consciously call on Dark entities, using certain secret rituals (or, in the modern-day, programming methods), and ask for their help. Such help always comes at a price, of course, for both the individuals and the world as a whole, and is never worth it for those who have a longer-term understanding. That's why it's often said such people "sell their souls to the devil."

How Representatives of Light Influence the World

Similarly, emissaries or servants of Light will follow a set of orders. However, these are the polar opposite of Dark tenets; altruism (service to others), allowing individuals to ascend at their own pace, respecting individual freedoms, and so on. Here is a list of characteristics Light-influenced beings will typically exhibit.

- **Increasing freedom:** Teachers, preachers, and occasionally leaders of Light will try to liberate others from slavery (physical, mental, and spiritual) and organize society along lines that maximize opportunities for individuals to actualize themselves and their abilities. Light ideals allow people to worship as they see fit as long as they don't try to oppress others, allowing people to marry and make friends with anyone they choose (i.e. reducing racial discrimination), and allowing them to travel and live wherever they want as opposed to tying them to the land like serfs.

- **God sends many teachers:** Earth has seen many great and influential beings that helped Humanity at crossroads. These beings served as inventors, authors, teachers, gods/goddesses, enlightened beings, and spiritual masters. We will talk about one such great being Christ (born as Jesus Christ) in future chapters. How this iconic being changed much of the course of human history.

- **Growing along with others:** The Universal Father preaches Service to Others—meaning that individuals should not care about making money or fame themselves and be focused more on helping others. This altruism means that Light gurus and teachers often live modest, even austere lives, with few (if any) material possessions, and rarely try to gain wealth or material goods for their purposes. Rather, they will almost always donate what they own to the poor and work their hardest to ensure the community as a whole, and those around them, are as happy and healthy as possible.

- **Spreading information:** Light teachers will never forbid anyone else from learning new things or seeking information. Instead, they will try to spread education and knowledge as far and wide as possible, whether by preaching, posting good articles on the Internet, teaching others to read, publishing books, and so on. They will also try to make the information as decentralized as possible so no individual or single large corporation can control it.

- **Encouraging free thought:** Servants of Light know that everyone has their path to enlightenment and ascension to Heaven. A true servant of Light will also never claim to be perfect or some kind of infallible authority. Instead, they will tell you to cultivate your judgment and critical thinking and figure out the best ways to help others on your own. The knowledge and wisdom dispensed by Light acolytes merely serve as a guidepost or form of assistance rather than a straitjacket.

- **Creating positive karma:** The forces of Light want

humans to generate positive karma so they can become worthy of higher levels of consciousness rather than being trapped in one's minds. In addition to this being good for individuals, it also creates positive vibratory energy that strengthens the forces of Light.

- **Learn dark tactics:** It is quite common to see some light warrior beings change robes to the other side. This is to get a first-hand experience from the inside.

- **DNA manipulation:** As mentioned above, certain portions of DNA contain knowledge on how to ascend closer to God—even if individuals cannot access memories in most circumstances, on occasion, their DNA can give them revelations that can help them without conscious knowledge. While the Dark wants to cut such genetics out of human society, the Light wants to increase its frequency and spread them as far as possible. Thus, Light will either use scientific knowledge to edit DNA and put very useful genetic information inside individual humans (never without their consent, of course) or try to manipulate bloodlines. Sometimes 'Cupids' will help people fall in love or find their soulmates if they have special DNA, allowing that DNA to mix and spread in their children and allowing larger segments of the human population to enjoy the benefits of Light genetics.

- **Truthfulness:** When it comes to history, they will use the most painstaking and rigorous methodology, never glossing over the bad parts or tragedies of the past and never exaggerating the good parts or triumphs either. They will never censor historical records or try to blot them out, but they will always try to ensure what really happens gets told for the benefit of future generations. By the same token, while religion contains some wisdom, by extension, none of them contain the whole truth—servants of Light will never try to blot out religious truths and never use them for their own ends. Instead, they will always work together with all people and attempt to find the higher spiritual truths

- **Handing out virtuous knowledge:** Finally, servants of Light will always be happy to tell you how you can live a better, more virtuous life on your terms, without forcing you to do anything. They will give suggestions on emotional health, how to volunteer your time and donate to charity, and so on.

How Light and Dark Evolve

T here are many levels of consciousness in the universe, with a myriad number of teachers. Based on your level of soul growth, a teacher works with you to help you progress to the next level of your soul's journey. You will find that as you progress on your evolutionary journey, the teachers change too. It is said when the student is ready, the teacher appears. There are possibly infinite levels of growth potential, as there are an infinite number of experiences for the soul. Christ has alluded to multiple levels of Heaven when He said:

> "In My Father's house are many rooms. If it were not so, would I have told you that I am going there to prepare a place for you? " – John 14:2

Schools of Light

Think of the education of young people for a moment—in this example, we'll use the United States of America, but any other country will probably have something similar. In this country, there are elementary schools—kindergarten, first grade, all the way up to fifth grade—then middle school, for grades six to eight. After that is high school, up to twelfth grade, and then finally, at the age of eighteen, a child is sent off to college, where they spend four years getting a bachelor's degree. Then, finally, you have the most advanced courses of study in graduate school, where an adult can learn the most complicated and esoteric subjects to gain a master's degree— or even a full doctorate—indicating he or she has absolutely mastered a field of study and contributed original knowledge to it!

The cosmic hierarchy is incredibly and meticulously organized. The angels are teachers and professors to other angels, as well as evolving souls, in ways very similar to how we have elementary school teachers, high school teachers, and college professors, all the way up to supervisors of graduate dissertations. On earth or Urantia as it is also called—the education of our souls in our daily lives can be analogized to about third grade of complexity and difficulty. The more the soul evolves and the more wisdom it acquires, the higher level of spiritual education it can access.

It is difficult to describe exactly how this happens—it is one of those mysteries very few people on earth, even the very wisest, are privy to. Despite all my hours of research and study, I only have the very basics down. But from what I have researched, this jump-started education happens when you are asleep. If you have had a stress-free day and you're able to have a very comfortable sleep in a state of mind that is serene and prepared for restfulness, higher realities might be able to beam information into your brain using dreams and visions. After all great inventions on Earth have been through Dreams and Visions.

Many souls have individual guides from higher levels of consciousness— much like sometimes in our world, distinguished college professors might take an interest in child prodigies. In these cases, the great professors of heavenly reals will enter your dreams and give you knowledge that helps your soul grow. In many cases, you might not even realize it—you won't remember your dreams when you wake up, but you will greet the day with a more serene demeanor, more patience, and a better ability to overcome any problems you encounter and treat others with benevolence. Other times, you might remember the dream and the exact words your spiritual guide told you! And sometimes, the guides will subtly influence you in your waking hours, allowing you to be more perceptive and enhance your memories. This is a plan enacted by the forces of Light called "Deep Learning," to strengthen souls who might be particularly useful in the campaign against Satan in the future.

Evolution of Darkness

As scary as it might sound, Satan and his forces of Darkness also seem to be able to evolve and strengthen themselves. I know even less about this than I do about the evolution of Light-aligned souls. Satan and his minions are very secretive, and it can be very dangerous to try to infiltrate their spiritual zones, the systems under their control, and the secret societies they have on Earth. However, if the forces of Darkness were completely unable to evolve, they would have lost the war long ago, and the struggle for the earth would not be as important.

Lucifer's agenda is to be a creator that rivals God. He used artificial and spiritual means to create higher evolutionary beings. His method included both artificial and natural means coupled with his own spirit to create souls.

Lucifer's servants do not want human souls to ascend to heaven or higher vibratory levels and, thus, cut themselves and those bound to them off from the great teachings of Heaven. Indeed, it is doubtful whether darkness has any analogous learning methods. However, through his control of politicians, CEOs, and other influential leaders on earth, and through the efforts of the Princes on the worlds and angels who swore loyalty to him 200,000 years ago, Lucifer has created research institutions on worlds under his dominion. I am certain the Dark has a methodical hierarchical structure just like the lighted realms. An example, a mind-controlled person can go on a rampage and kill many innocent children; this person is promised an elevated position in the dark circles. This sort of thing happens at an unconscious level and the physically bodied human is not aware. Remember we are multi-dimensional beings.

Higher dark beings know more about light than average humans. These higher dark beings serve outwardly as good teachers of religion, but they ultimately take all their followers to hell or get them killed. We have seen many examples of cults that fall into this category on Earth. There are many well-known teachers/preachers in our world today that fall into this category. How will you know or recognize it? Not easy. Remember the main weapon of Satan is "Deception". Your only weapon in these situations is to trust your intuition.

No one currently knows where these Dark laboratories are located; finding them is a crucial task for agents of Light in the coming conflict. However, at these hidden 'lodges' as they are called, Satan strengthens his minions both consciously and unconsciously.

BESTOWAL OF CHRIST THE FIRST COMING

V irtually everyone in the world, religious or not, has heard of Jesus Christ. Christians believe he was the Son of God, while Muslims believe he was a great prophet. Even atheists express approval of his moral teachings, regardless of whether they acknowledge the existence of the divine or spiritual realities. Unfortunately, the forces of Darkness have worked as hard as they possibly can, to distort and obscure the true teachings of Jesus, because he was and is the greatest force in the entire universe standing against their plans, and will play a crucial role in the final battle against Satan here on Earth.

It is very sad to acknowledge that so much rancor has been caused— and in many cases, blood spilled—over esoteric matters like which particular church out of thousands is closest to the truth, what the precise ritual of the Christian Mass should entail, and so on. The most important things were always Christ's teachings of love, altruism, and devotion to the Divine. Fortunately, this book will reveal to you how things happened, and the specific ways in which Christ will fight Satan, regardless of what any particular religion says about rituals or the so-called 'correct' way to worship God.

Planet Earth is absolutely central to the battle between Light and Dark due to the comparatively massive amount of spiritual energy human beings produce. And while the struggle was slow, Satan was slowly but surely gaining the upper hand through a variety of means. His agents surreptitiously eliminated Light bloodlines on Earth, subverted the noble teachings of many great philosophers like Aristotle or Zoroaster, and placed merciless conquerors in positions of power (across the Roman empire, for instance) to keep humanity mired in war and oppression, preventing many of us from evolving and growing closer to the Light. It was getting harder and harder for agents of Light to access the planet, very few people could commune with the Universal Father at all, and the Dark had succeeded in turning many unfortunate human souls into perpetual energy batteries, fueling the campaign against God. These troubling developments drew the attention of not just God but the highest of His angels who had been charged with overseeing our universe.

In our universe, this process became harder on Earth due to the spiritual Matrix having been spread over it. On the other hand, the forces of Light absolutely could not allow

Earth to fall into the Dark, or else everything would be lost. Thus, Christ embarked upon the riskiest and most dangerous plan imaginable for an angel of his stature. He would undergo Bestowal and use all of his energies to penetrate the Matrix. However, due to the extreme cost of that procedure, Christ would appear on Earth not as a full-grown adult, but as a humble child, profoundly vulnerable to the many Dark forces seeking his destruction!

Christ is the creator of our universe. The best way to know about His creation is to be part of the creation. By the agreement with the Trinity consciousness, Christ decided to incarnate and be part of His Creation. Upon completing His bestowal, He will be the ultimate authority of all of His creation. Now, this bestowal can happen as a full-fledged being with all powers intact or in any way He chooses. This was essentially Christ first coming. This was a completely secret mission between God and Christ, not even the angles and arch angels in Paradise were aware. Only after His birth as a helpless small baby, the announcement went out to the entire headquarters of the Universe in heavenly realms. Angels were surprised as He did not bestow with powers intact but as a helpless babe. And yes, the baby is subjected to all rules of the Matrix.

While there are many ways the first-coming mission can be interpreted, the primary purpose is to help Light win the war.

For Christ, the rewards were worth the risks. If he managed to grow to adulthood on Earth, this Bestowal would prove for all time that he was truly a gifted creator and administrator and that he deserved to be sovereign over his universe for all eternity. And not only that, but success in this mission would pave the way for Light's victory, as it would undo much of the progress Dark had made in subverting human society and turning people into Dark strongholds. Indeed, such a triumph would liberate not only Earth but also the Universe in general. This would lead to a cascade effect, where Satan's forces would subsequently grow weaker day after day, and the forces of Light grow stronger at the same rate, allowing a swift end to the entire Rebellion after the final battle on Earth. So incredibly important was this operation that it was kept secret from even the other angels. No one knew what God and Christ were planning until he had arrived— or more accurately, been born—on Earth!

And then, for about thirty years, all eyes across the entire universe were intently focused on this one small corner of it, watching the greatest drama in millions of years unfold.

You might be able to realize it by now: The date of Christ's Bestowal on Earth was 0 AD, and he was incarnated as a humble Jewish baby from Bethlehem. He grew up to be a great teacher, miracle worker, and prophet. Now, religious scholars reading this book, and devout church-goers might be uneasy with this description of Christ's birth and his relationship with God. Even if you can't believe this account, it's far more important for you to understand Christ's moral teachings rather than the theology and metaphysics behind his bestowal. Indeed, such things are nearly impossible for ordinary humans to understand, even the most enlightened of us unless we ascend very high in the spiritual hierarchy–a process which would take much longer than our time on earth.

Christ's Mission on Earth

It is beyond the scope of this book to dive deep into Christ's life and teachings in the Matrix. A brief account here.

During his lifetime, Jesus was known as Joshua ben Joseph; as Christ accepted the naming conventions of the Jewish community in which he incarnated–Joseph was the father of Jesus, and in Hebrew, "ben" means "Son Of ". Despite Satan's best attempts, most of Jesus' teachings, though not all, were faithfully preserved throughout the four Gospels. As one of the primary reasons for Christ to appear on Earth was to demonstrate a Godly life by example, the kindness Christ showed to the poor and needy and the virtuous acts he performed taught many in his mortal lifetime how to be more like the Universal Father, and they are still very useful lessons today.

The Sermon on the Mount is perhaps the most concise and perceptive description of the ideals of Light to be found in the Bible As described previously in this book, Light emphasizes altruism while Dark emphasizes selfishness. In these passages from Matthew, Jesus told us that the poor, meek, righteous, merciful, and needy are blessed; Satan would say the opposite, that the proud, avaricious, and ruthlessly self-interested are superior. He told us to control our anger and let go of grudges and negative emotions. He also told us not to retaliate with cruelty to even those who have been cruel to us; instead, pray that they may turn from the path of evil. He also told us not to worry about even significant things, but to cultivate calmness and self-assuredness even in the face of adversity, and not to hoard massive amounts of wealth but instead give it to the unfortunate and spend it to better our communities.

The ultimate aim of all this, of course, was to find "The Father within" and have a personal relationship with Him. Also to "*give glory to your Father in heaven*" (English Standard Version Bible, 2001, Matt. 5.1-29). By practicing altruism and forgiveness, not only will you help those around you and strengthen your community, but you will make your soul purer and clearer. While you are alive, you will be better attuned to higher realities and it will be easier for you to access them– and even guidance from agents of Light–in dreams. When you die, if you have lived according to Christ's precepts, it will be much easier for your soul to ascend to a higher vibratory level, perhaps even allowing you entry into one of the higher heavenly realms where you can learn the secrets of the Divine from skilled angels!

Curing Diseases and Driving Out Demons: This is fairly self-explanatory. The numerous supernatural acts Christ performed, which were always done in a spirit of love and helping human beings, were to prove that Light still held power even in a world entrapped within the Matrix and that Christ himself possessed awesome power that made him worthy of ruling our universe. All this, of course, also attested to the Universal Father from whom Christ's authority and powers derived. Examples of these events are Christ's healing of the Canaanite woman, producing enough fish and bread from a small amount to feed a whole crowd of people, and driving away many demons–servants of Satan–who possessed people he came across and even walking on water.

Jesus Rejects Satan

Perhaps the greatest miracle of all that Christ performed, and arguably the most important—though even Biblical scholars and learned clergymen might be surprised to hear this—was his rejection of Satan in the wilderness. Some texts attribute this to happening on Mount Hermon. For all his, truly impressive miracles and the indisputably marvelous moral example, he set for all of mankind during the time he spent on Earth, his direct confrontation with the leader of Darkness dealt a massive blow to his plans and gave Light a path to victory on Earth, and thus possibly saved the entire universe from Lucifer rebellion if the final battle on Earth is successful.

Satan had been waging his rebellion for many thousands of years, and he was a very crafty, intelligent commander indeed. If he were not, Light would have won a very long time ago! So just as Christ came up with a plan to save Earth, Satan came up with a plan to not only capture it himself, but perhaps destroy the forces of Light in the material world, and then onwards throughout the rest of the universe.

Bestowed on Earth as a human being, Christ is directly connected to the Universal Father and possesses astonishing supernatural powers–still tied Christ down to the physical universe, with all the limitations that implied. The Matrix prevented him from using all of his spiritual powers. Additionally, human beings are physical creatures who evolved over a long period and have not reached our highest levels of development. So being incarnated as a humble Jewish boy in a much more primitive period meant Christ possessed many of the same weaknesses human beings in general do. He had to deal with physical deprivations like hunger and thirst, his human will was not as strong as it was when he was reigning as a great angel, and so on. In other words, the all-too-human Jesus, the savior of Earth could himself be tempted, and possibly turned over to the side of Darkness!

If you have already read the Bible, you are probably already familiar with how this story goes. In the gospels of Matthew, Mark, and Luke, we have a reliable account of Jesus entering the wilderness outside of the cities, where "the devil"--not named in the text, but we know he was Satan–gave him a battery of tests and false offers.

For instance, He was challenged to demonstrate his divine powers by turning rocks into bread, but Jesus refused since he had no reason to take orders from the unrepentant fallen angel.

Mathew 4:3 And the tempter came and said to him, *"If you are the Son of God, command these stones to become loaves of bread."*

Then Satan teleported both of them to the highest point in Jerusalem, the top of its largest temple, and told Jesus that ownership of the whole world would be his if he joined the forces of Darkness. Fortunately for the entire universe, of course, Jesus declined.

Satan came up with a wide variety of proposals, using every bit of skill and cunning he had as a negotiator. In response, Jesus resolutely remained loyal to the Universal Father.

"If you are the Son of God, throw yourself down, for it is written, "'He will command his angels concerning you,' and "'On their hands they will bear you up, lest you strike your foot against a stone.'" - Mathew 4:6

After this refusal, Satan tried to offer a series of compromises, each more seemingly favorable than the last, but Jesus rejected each and every one of them with the simple phrase, "the will of my Father in Paradise be done." At long last, completely frustrated and defeated, Satan tried to threaten Jesus directly, but he declared "get thee behind me" and drove Satan away, sending him fleeing far from Earth.

In many ways, this was the defining moment. This was a defining moment for Christ also in addition to the war itself. If Satan was successful in tempting Christ, planet

Earth would have fallen already. Christ was feeble and weak from hunger. Satan's timing was perfect. Christ stood strong in His relationship with the Father and prevailed. During this ordeal, the Father was not present as Christ had to pass this test of his own volition. He did pass this crucial test and Father re-joined with Christ.

This was a defining moment as this incident gave temporary victory to light over the dark. According to Urantia's book, the reigning planetary prince of Earth "Caligastia", was cast out of his throne. Caligastia is no longer the planetary prince. Christ in addition to being the creator of the Universe, also took over the role of the planetary prince. The Bible verse states this:

> "Now is the judgment of this world; now shall the prince of this world (Caligastia) be cast down." – John 12:31

And then still nearer the completion of His lifework, He announced,

> "The prince of this world (Caligastia) is judged." – John 16:11

This was the purpose of the Bestowal. By proving he was immune to Satan's temptations, even as a fallible and vulnerable human being, Christ proved he was also worthy to rule over planet Earth justly and wisely and thus oversee the entire universe with the same integrity and prudence. And by driving Satan away, Jesus had stalled–though not completely halted–the advance of Darkness on this most valuable planet, giving the forces of Light plenty of time to prepare for the final battle in the future.

Jesus Christ became the planetary prince and sole commander of Earth as well as all universe. Earth would become a throne world of Light, once final victory is achieved.

This event is the single most important event in the history of Earth. As stated above if Christ had failed, Earth would have been in perpetual darkness. I go into great detail about how this battle played out in my book "Son of Man becomes Son of God". There is a link to this book if you are interested to learn more.

Jesus Chooses Love

Finally, to really understand the importance of the Bestowal, you have to understand precisely how Christ beat Satan. It was not through physical power, obviously, but neither was it through spiritual power alone, even though Christ had more than enough of it. It was instead through the power of love.

Christ could have become the wealthiest, most powerful man on Earth through the miracles he performed. He could have dethroned every general and emperor on the planet at the time–and could still do so today if he desired. Yet he explicitly chose not to, even when Satan offered him the opportunity, and even when others mocked him by saying

"He saved others; himself he cannot save"—because he would not" (136:6.5).

Satan and Lucifer may have been too short-sighted to perceive the strength of Christ's example, but the rest of the universe—and hopefully humanity—were not. Christ proved to the legions of other angels, extraterrestrial and extra-universal beings, and other observers who were watching events on Earth that using one's talents and abilities for mere personal aggrandizement is utterly futile and self-defeating. Higher values, like intellectual development, spiritual achievement, and altruism, earning one the genuine–rather than forced–love and devotion of others in one's community, are worth infinitely more than purely physical benefits like wealth, temporal power, or even health. Thus, all of creation, angels, and humans alike should focus on intellectual and spiritual advancement to grow closer to the absolute apex of mind and spirit: The Universal Father Himself.

The lyrics for the song fit well in this context:

Light of the world, You stepped down into darkness

Opened my eyes, Let me see

Beauty that made this heart adore You

Hope of a life spent with You

And here I am to worship, Here I am to bow down

Here I am to say that You're my God You're altogether lovely Altogether worthy Altogether wonderful to me

King of all days, Oh, so highly exalted Glorious in heaven above, Humbly You came To the earth You created

All for love's sake became poor

– Here I Am To Worship (songwriter: Tim Hughes)

BENEFITS FROM LUCIFER REBELLION - GOOD FROM EVIL

R eading about Satan's rebellion against God is surely a harrowing experience. While Christ brought the universe valuable time and greatly hindered Satan's plans, it is still very distressing to know that the forces of darkness have not been banished completely and that Satan's minions are still enslaving souls, suppressing freedom, and infiltrating governments even today. Collective consciousness is treated like sheep, with almost no free will.

It is understandable if even devout people of the Earth might find their faith in the Universal Father wavering somewhat. Why would God allow this rebellion to last for so long and spread so far?

How could He allow Satan's army to cause so much misery? There are answers to these questions, though even great sages did not realize them at first. This chapter will explore how Satan, arrogant and haughty and utterly in love with his self-perceived superiority, actually aided God's plans in the long run through his terrible rebellion.

The Truth Will Set You Free

First is the fact that God never abrogated humanity's free will-or that of any other species in the universe, including

His angels. Lucifer/Satan was allowed to rebel against God, and human beings are allowed to sell themselves into servitude to his forces. However, imagine what it would be like if this were not so. Freedom of choice is what allows humans, aliens, angels, and other sentient beings to truly grow. If God just forced all creatures to serve Him, with no choice in the matter, they would not really be sentient, but instead, merely androids or dolls that God was playing with. God does not want mere toys. He wants true companions to join Him on His journey of creation. It is important to note that your spirit is part of God and in some ways, your experience is God's experience and God's experience is your experience. And for that reason, giving His creatures the choice to rebel or not, even if they make the wrong choices as Lucifer did, was necessary to produce a universe where the struggles and tribulations of its inhabitants had meaning.

This is particularly true for humans on Earth. We play a central role in Satan's rebellion, which he was not able to foresee, even though he eventually adapted his plans to our unique circumstances and had great success before Christ's Bestowal. God realizes our importance as well, but He still has not penetrated the Matrix surrounding our world and simply enlisted us all to the cause of Light. If He did that, He would have been no better than Satan, who seeks to enslave others and bend them to his will, denying their free choice. Instead, human beings have been given the opportunity for nearly unrestricted freedom of expression, even as we are watched over and guided by heavenly agents of Light. Even as we struggle against the Dark, even as some fail, or worse, join Satan of their own free will, we prove that we are sentient individuals interacting with the universe on our terms, with our hopes and dreams and joys. The context of Satan's rebellion allows our struggles to have meaning and attest to both our accomplishments and the greater glory of God in ways Satan, utterly selfish and blind to the value of freedom in and of itself, could never understand.

Duality

Satan's rebellion also upholds the contrast between Light and Dark, through which, ironically enough, Light can achieve great things even as the Dark spitefully tries to undermine it. Satan's rebellion can serve as a teaching example–in a negative sense–for individual mortal souls, showing them the sorts of pitfalls to avoid on their path to enlightenment and higher realms of consciousness. By studying the reasons behind Satan's rebellion, the mistakes he made, and the traps he tries to set for seekers of truth, souls will find ascension to be that much easier. Indeed, many of the wisest human souls can consciously evolve through Darkness itself! Just like Jesus at Mount Hermon proved his virtue and his right to rule by rejecting Satan, those wise warriors of Light in the human world, by consciously and bravely staring down the Dark, strengthen their souls and can easily pass on to a higher vibratory level in one's lifetime.

On that note, redemption is also a powerful source of energy for God's servants. In previous chapters, we described how the Dark wants to entrap human souls to use as batteries, while the Light gains energy from the growth and progression of those souls. The greatest kind of progression, however, is not a normal human rising to a higher plane after a virtuous life, but a human tainted by darkness learning from their mistakes, shedding Satan's evil entrapments, and returning to the Light. To use the technical language, 'transmuting' Darkness to Light produces more power than a soul that simply ascends constantly within the Light alone–though that isn't a bad thing either.

Many angels, while still loyal to the Universal Father–or at least not opposing Him or supporting Satan–still do not understand the point of actively fighting the rebellion. They have not taken up any tasks related to the duality of Light and Dark, trying to be neutral. This is a free choice of theirs, and God has not abrogated it either. However, these neutral angels are 'missing out on a huge part of what makes living in the multiverse meaningful. They not only avoid the war within lower universes—that is to say, they do not try to guide material beings on Earth or elsewhere fighting Satan—but they obviously have not incarnated themselves as material beings through Bestowals. Thus, they lack empathy for the "lower" beings and do not understand what it means to have a limited consciousness. These angels find it somewhat more difficult to advance in the celestial hierarchy due to lacking such virtues.

Rebellion-resistant civilization

Another long-term benefit of Satan's rebellion is the production of a civilization built on conscious loyalty to God and thus more resistant to subversion than any that came before it. God, as loving and compassionate as He is, realizes that living under the shadow of Darkness is extremely difficult for mortals. He understands and sympathizes with our pain, honoring the many sacrifices we have made throughout the war and crying with us as we mourn for souls lost to darkness and the many lives needlessly cut short by war, chaos, slavery, and other assorted types of misery Satan and his agents spread across Earth. But as the old saying goes, 'no pain, no gain.' All these trials strengthen humanity and thus the cause of Light in the long run.

By forcing us to face the misery caused by the rebellion 'up close and personal,' so to speak, humans gain first-hand knowledge of what is at stake in the war and why the darkness must be defeated. This makes us much more determined to fight for the right side and much more willing to make sacrifices for the cause, which even higher angels aren't always willing to make. Also, conflict on Earth serves as a "testing ground" for Light strategies, allowing loyal angels to watch and see where the strengths and weaknesses of both sides are, what tactics are most effective against the Dark, and which ones ought to be abandoned. Wise humans who are aware of the conflict and participate in it become 'veterans' and when they progress on to Heaven, become much more effective soldiers against Darkness in the future.

At the end of the conflict, then, after humans have been seasoned by the constant struggle against the rebellion, the forces of Light will have an entire planet full of tough soldiers with the utmost determination to fight against Dark. These seasoned veterans will reform Earth's societies to create an entire civilization highly resistant to further subversion. After so much time, money, and effort spent on the Rebellion, Earth's people will know every trick and scheme in the Darkness playbook from top to bottom and will be able to resist them very easily. Earthlings will be effectively 'inoculated' against the possibility of further dark rebellions in the universe.

Even better, Earth will have set an example for the rest of the universe. Countless human veterans of the conflicts will pass on their knowledge and skills as they ascend to higher planes, teaching and guiding both their descendants–through dreams–and other residents of the universe who are fighting on other worlds. This wisdom will be passed on for all eternity, never to be forgotten. And finally, by allowing those who have fallen to Darkness to redeem themselves, reject their former mistakes, and rejoin the side of light, humans will know how to draw Satan's misguided servants back onto the side of righteousness. In other words, the rebellion has offered Light the opportunity to test a variety of methods for the 'transmutation' of Darkness to Light. Once the most effective method has been chosen, agents from Earth will spread this information all across the universe, providing all of creation with the ultimate tool in the toolbox for spiritual advancement–because, as we discussed, turning Darkness to Light creates more positive spiritual energy than nearly anything else.

New Physical Angels

All this is to prepare humanity to become something unique, something is never seen before throughout the entire history of the universe: Physical angels. Unlike all other kinds of angels, which did not start as material creatures–only becoming so after undergoing Bestowal–humans started as physical, material creatures undergoing natural evolution, but after Darkness is defeated, we have a chance to ascend through the power of Light and become angels ourselves, much like those beings which have been watching over us for millennia. This new species of physical angels will be even more powerful and virtuous than all the other angelic orders, due to having been strengthened by the struggle against Darkness throughout our mortal lifespans.

This is the meaning of Christ's words from the Bible: "So the last will be first, and the first last" (English Standard Version Bible, 2001, Matt. 20:16). Lucifer was the first of God's mightiest angels, unmatched in his power, skill, and intelligence. He was a top-notch administrator who earned the respect of all of his colleagues. Yet he lost sight of what was truly important and grew drunk on his arrogance, haughtiness, and pride. Thus, he rebelled against his Creator, losing everything he had previously earned and becoming a villain on the stage of the universe. If agents of the Light are successful in the final battle, Lucifer and his cohorts will have no chance of victory and will be utterly cast down and humbled. In other words, the first of the angels will become the very last. On the other hand, human beings started as the lowliest, most humble beings in all of creation. We arose on a small planet at the very edge of a small galaxy in a universe not particularly important within the epic scheme of the universe. And yet, due to a combination of luck and design, our souls produce so much energy for both Light and Dark that we became the ultimate prize in the titanic cosmic struggle between Light and Dark, and if Light wins, we have the chance to become the most powerful angels of all. That is a huge benefit of Lucifer's rebellion, one he did not foresee or intend: Humans were the last, but we might become the first.

Lion Will Lay Down with the Lamb

The dark forces by nature are aggressive. Most of the authoritative positions are held by Dark brothers and sisters. They are like the Lion. In contrast, human beings are meek and sheep-like easily manipulated by Higher-level dark beings. It is expected that there will be peace and that Lion will lay down with Lamb after Christ second coming thereby bringing much-needed balance on Earth and to the local sector of the Universe.

Deeper and richer experiences

There are great historical records of everything meticulously maintained in the Universe by dedicated record keepers. The rich and varied experiences that humanity and Earth brings adds incredible value to the universe. The entire experience of all souls and planets is recorded. This serves as teaching material to knowledge/wisdom seekers. These records will include the war and all the chess games being played over thousands of years. This is rich information in the annals of history. We are creating this very day.

There are millions of angelic beings across the universe observing intently chess games being played on a daily basis. However, most of us are completely unaware and have no knowledge or insight into any of this. This is exactly as dark forces designed. Remember the main weapon of darkness is deception.

Methods of Growth

Linear Growth

Now, there are two ways this sort of growth can occur. The first, and much more common way, is to scale one level of skill or accomplishment at a time in a steady and linear fashion. We can roughly analogize this kind of growth to the education you might have received from early childhood to adolescence to adulthood. You start off in first grade (to take an American example), and as you get older, and thus wiser and smarter, you move up to the second, third, fourth, and fifth grades as the years pass by. With every increase in your academic grade, you are expected to solve tougher and tougher problems on your tests and homework and accept more and more responsibility in your daily life. Then you go to high school, and after that, you move on to college, where you can get your bachelor's degree. Then, if you are a very studious adult, you can go even further, and get a postgraduate degree, and eventually even a doctorate if you want to be an absolute expert in your field!

This is roughly the process individual souls both in the universe and in the angelic realms go through. Then, by studying God's teachings and contemplating His will, they become wiser and thus unlock higher spiritual realities. They continue this process over the course of their life, going up one level at a time, slowly but surely becoming more and more important to the machinations of the Light, and in many cases helping those on lower levels advance as they do.

Think of a Catholic monk who starts out as an initiate, then advances in the hierarchy of the Church until he has proven enough wisdom and discernment to become the abbot of his monastery, teaching and guiding the younger monks on their own paths. This steady, quantified model of spiritual advancement can be seen as an example of **linear growth**, where one's status in Light's hierarchy rises at a constant rate, not an exceedingly fast one.

Exponential Growth

However, there is another method of spiritual growth that is much faster. Indeed, it exhibits exponential growth. Exponential growth is when a quantifiable property (in this case, the measure of one's skill and wisdom within the Light) both increases on its own, *and* sees its *rate* of increase grow over time, so it grows faster and faster as it advances, leading to an incredibly fast rate of advancement. In layman's terms, this is a much faster way to grow than utilizing the basic linear model. But exponential spiritual growth requires the existence of evil and Darkness, which is why God has thus far allowed Satan to move forward with his schemes until the Second Coming.

To understand why this is so, you need to understand the complex relationship between Darkness and Light. Both elements of reality feed off of each other, in a way. All throughout this book, we have discussed how the Dark gains its greatest benefit from corrupting the Light. Satan is always trying to snuff out the most highly Light-attuned souls. And by destroying the faith or bringing down to Satan the most positive, pious, and God-fearing souls, a great deal of negative Dark energy is released, empowering Satan's armies.

But the opposite also holds. When a good person endures a great deal of personal hardship and becomes more charitable and altruistic because of it, they release a lot of Light energy, which strengthens God's forces. When someone casts out a demon from a possessed person with the power of their faith, Darkness is drained from Satan's reserves, and Light energy is given off. Negative occurrences like famines or disasters, whether natural, man-made, or demonically inspired, offer us chances to display Light virtues such as altruism and compassion. Indeed, it is logically impossible to display compassion without someone suffering misfortune, or heroism and courage without terrifying disasters to test our spirits. Those goods logically depend on those evils.

This applies on both an individual level and to Earth as a whole. A good person with an easy life will gradually ascend through the various tiers of Light, but only relatively slowly: The trajectory of their growth will remain constant, or linear, so they will achieve respectable heights but not truly stratospheric ones. However, if someone is assaulted gravely by Satan, or goes through many Dark experiences, it will undoubtedly be very difficult and painful for them, but their growth trajectory will vastly accelerate. In other words, someone who endures many trials set by Darkness rather than enjoying an easy but challenge-free life will be on an *exponential* trajectory of growth in their Light energy. This is partly because Light requires room to grow, and Darkness, being the opposite of Light, leaves an even more spacious vacuum for Light energies when it is banished. Thus, when one is plunged into the deepest depths of Darkness, you have the opportunity to carry much more Light, which explains the much faster growth when one overcomes Darkness and Dark-related challenges.

There is some truth in the saying, the deeper one falls into darkness, the greater is the potential of growth.

Just as those special, virtuous people who are like candles burning against the Darkness attract the lion's share of its attention, places that are gravely assailed by the Dark, or people desperately crying out for aid against it, also attract the Light. The two opposites attract each other, in other words. And while this effect is strong for individuals, when applied on a planetary scale it is vastly multiplied.

Yes, good reader, you have now arrived at the reason God and Christ have allowed Satan to achieve, temporarily, what seems like total dominion over the Earth. This entire planet, and all of us, its inhabitants, have been placed on that higher growth trajectory for Light precisely because we are suffering so much at the hands of the Dark. Make no mistake, Satan indeed has his evil claws stuck very deeply into our planet. Indeed, though his rebellion was cosmic in nature, no other planet in the entire universe is as embroiled in Darkness as ours is. Planet Earth is the epicenter of darkness in the universe. There is great mercy and grace by God, Christ, and all celestial beings for all Humans.

Though demons may harry the inhabitants of other worlds, they are focused on none other as keenly as Earth, and only on Earth have they been able to disrupt the astral plane so thoroughly that only a few of us are able to perceive it and learn from it—on other planets it is much easier to access the higher spiritual planes and commune with angels, and there is much less skepticism of the teachings of Light, and much more direct obedience of God than there is here. Earth, on the other hand, is embroiled in chaos and darkness that is worse than any of God's angels in Heaven have ever seen, despite the unimaginably long time they have spent fighting the Dark. No other planet has temples overtly dedicated to worshiping Satan, or powerful secret societies creating prisons of Darkness for the planet's own inhabitants, for instance. Yet precisely because reaching higher spiritual levels is so difficult for us, when we do succeed, our rewards are that much greater.

Tipping Point Reached in Today's World

We are living in the year 2023. Lucifer's rebellion started over two hundred thousand years ago, but even then, the forces of both Light and Dark realized that this timeframe 2020's would be very crucial for the resistance, though only the leaders of Light knew that it would be two thousand years after Christ's Bestowal on Earth as Jesus Christ.

Bluntly stated, that we are living in the last days just before the true final battle. I would not be able to tell you the exact time or date of that battle–such mysteries are beyond even the wisest humans who have ever lived. But life on Earth is definitely edging closer and closer to a tipping point, after which the conflict, previously unknown to the vast majority of human beings, will become over, and a victor will be decided once and for all. Both sides are marshaling their forces and trying to increase their influence in human society. Agents of Dark and Light are both more numerous and more active.

Not many may have noticed this. But this is due to the pervasive nature of the spiritual Matrix in which we live. Agent Smith, in the Hollywood movie, put it very aptly:

> "Have you ever stood and stared at it... marveled at its beauty? Billions of people, just living out their lives... oblivious."

There is a full-blown attack currently underway on the general population of this planet as Dark armies go all out in defense of their very existence as they feel cornered and threatened. They are both on and off the planet. The full brunt of the effects is taking its toll on the human psyche. And their aim is the total and complete annihilation of the human race.

Smith was speaking to Neo, one of the very few people, in the context of the movie, who was aware of the Matrix and how it was used to enslave human beings to the service of machines. Agent Smith's quote can apply just as well to real life. The spiritual matrix, in its own way, is an astonishing accomplishment. It masks higher realities so perfectly that billions of human beings, not only today but throughout our history, live, work, and play while having absolutely no idea that angels and demons are battling ferociously all around them. They are all utterly oblivious. But this ignorance will not last forever. More and more humans are 'waking up' every day. There are great souls whose purpose is to hold the light fort strong, most are unknown and work behind the scenes, and you will possibly never see them in the media or public.

The culmination of the Plans of both Light and Dark

This truly is a total war in every sense of the word. Trillions of beings across our universe give their energies to one side or the other, and trillions upon trillions of beings across the entire universe build upon their efforts. Angels of Light work ceaselessly to protect and guide as many humans as they can, while shadowy masters of Darkness work equally hard to enslave as many people as possible, generate energy for Dark-aligned creatures, and cast Earth further and further into dark clutches.

Unless you are very lucky, you probably have not witnessed any of this with your own eyes, and even after reading this far, you might not believe such a massive struggle is really occurring. After all, it's easy to understand war is going on when you can see explosions, smell gunpowder in the air, and watch buildings being destroyed, missiles turning great swathes of land into smoking craters, and dead bodies appear all over a battlefield. But there aren't any angels or demons showing up on the TV anywhere. How can this be? Through the spiritual Matrix, of course. This veil around Earth makes both angels and Dark spirits invisible and also limits the direct interaction they can have with human beings. For the most part, they cannot intervene in our world physically, they can only appear when directly summoned by those with knowledge, or sometimes in dreams and even more rarely in visions.

Some people who can access higher realities through dreams, or to whom angels have appeared in visions, have been the leaders of the struggle throughout history even as they have worked in the shadows, and they will be crucial in the final battle that is approaching. This is a concept that is much easier for even the uneducated to grasp. Anyone with even a passing familiarity with 'mundane' world history– the sort taught in schools and colleges–knows how important a single person can be at the right place and at the right time. Jesus Christ, of course, is the first name that comes to mind. A single person living two thousand years ago started a spiritual revolution that had a massive impact on the rest of humanity! But there are plenty of other examples too. Martin Luther King, despite his humble beginnings, spearheaded a civil rights movement that changed the course of American history. Inventors like Einstein and Tesla have pretty much made the modern world, with their intellectual accomplishments allowing humans to explore space and communicate with each other from thousands of miles away. There are also, unfortunately, negative examples—people like Adolf Hitler have caused more misery, chaos, and destruction in a single lifetime than even thousands of evil individuals could cause.

What applies to the history we're all familiar with also applies to the hidden conflict between Light and Dark. It is always very few who have made the greatest difference. Unsung individual heroes of Light leading the charge for the rest of us, building up forces in important areas, and setting up strong points for the final battle. They are doing all they can to preserve human freedom and prevent Satan from turning all of us into slaves. And unknown servants of Darkness, using evil powers to gain more and more influence over the world without anyone else noticing, so that these few individuals can not only profit immensely but serve as great lieutenants in Satan's army when he finally makes his move. It is these few individuals–and I cannot claim to know their identities; both sides do their best to keep them secret–who shape the course of the final battle; the masses of humanity fighting on both sides can only follow the plans they have set.

Plans are coming together

The climax of these secret struggles is close at hand. Who will end up winning? That depends on a huge variety of different factors. On the one hand, Dark is constantly evolving and refining its tactics to cause as much destruction as possible, both physically and spiritually. Satan's officers are trying to assassinate human heroes of Light, and drive away–or even suborn to the Dark–angels and other Light beings assigned to protect them. On higher spiritual planes, evil demons are constantly ambushing angels, trying to directly destroy as many of God's soldiers as possible so fewer of them can participate in the final battle when the time comes. These spiritual and physical battles are also affecting the health of our dear Mother Earth itself, shaping the battlefield in the future.

Spiritually, Dark forces are trying to disrupt and poison the auras and spiritual energies of the soil, the plants, and the animals of our planet. Even though non-sentient beings do not have anywhere near the spiritual power thinking human beings do, they have a small degree of it, and it affects the spiritual health of humans as well. When the environment and lower living creatures have negative auras, it mutates the spirits of humans who eat those plants and animals or live around them, making it harder for the Light to reach them. And obviously, by physically poisoning the land, and releasing all kinds of pollutants into the atmosphere, the forces of Dark sicken and weaken humans. By spreading suffering among our kind, Darkness weakens our resistance to it and spreads its influence.

On the other hand, the forces of Light are always trying to preserve and spread favorable strands of DNA, so individuals possessing these genes can spread knowledge and power among the forces of good and lead the way in the final battle. Angels are also trying to help as many human souls as possible to evolve, both out of altruism and also because the process generates spiritual energy for Light. They also aid Light-aligned humans on Earth in foiling various evil plans launched by Satan's officers, ranging from stopping wars and saving lives to disrupting Dark rituals attempting to contact more powerful Satan's minions and severing connections Satan has to Earth.

Both sides are maintaining a very fine balance. If the struggle were to tip over too much to one side or another, the spiritual veil or Matrix would already have been shredded and we would see evidence of the conflict very clearly today. There may be an informal agreement between Light and Dark not to go too far with their plans.

It is certainly not a truce or ceasefire, but it is a limitation on the tactics both sides are allowed to deploy, sort of like if two nuclear-armed countries were to go to war, but both of them agreed beforehand not to launch their nukes and fight only with conventional forces. We have very little knowledge of what has gone on in all those meetings 'upstairs' so to speak but all we know is that both sides are holding much of their forces in reserve until the final battle arrives at last.

Dark Getting Desperate

Even if neither side is willing to use its most powerful weapons, the spiritual and physical weapons they are currently deploying still have the power to obliterate the entire planet if one side were to get really desperate. This is what is happening on the Dark side right now, both on Earth and elsewhere. The Dark is starting to attack large population centers in defense of its existence, as Satan grows more and more frustrated with the slow advance of his plans, even if he has been making steady gains. On Earth, Satan would like to completely and totally annihilate the human race if he cannot enslave us. While he could use his agents to convince the rulers of our world to start a deadly nuclear war, Satan's preferred weapon for our extermination is much more subtle. Their true nature is a mystery, but Dark forces have created certain terrible machines that can disintegrate human consciousness without leaving any trace of their activity, like bullets or chemicals. These machines can put people into comas or cause heart attacks and strokes for seemingly no reason.

Satan would like nothing better than to launch an all-out assault with these machines, causing billions of people in big cities across the globe to literally drop dead, and sending billions of others into comas where they would waste away over time. Only the heroic actions of Light-aligned heroes have prevented this desperate, last-ditch plan from succeeding. However, even as he threatens to slaughter mankind, Satan is persistent enough that if his machines are sabotaged, he will continue to try and enslave humans to work towards winning the final battle.

One reason benevolent forces have to work so hard to stop Satan's machines is that modern-day human beings are uniquely vulnerable. This is because the modern world is particularly unbalanced between science and spirituality. If we were not, we could more easily study spiritual energies and thus figure out where Satan's most powerful machines were, how they operated, and how we could defend against them and subsequently destroy them. However, since we tend to research only material science, we have almost no ability to study devices that threaten us on a spiritual level as well.

This is not to downplay or dismiss the effects and benefits of physical science. As described earlier, inventors like Einstein and Tesla have greatly aided the cause of Light by allowing us to communicate over greater distances, reach new horizons in space, and so on, and so forth. However, comparatively little attention has been paid to the spiritual rather than physical health of our species. Few scientists study consciousness, the evolution of the soul, communication with angels, defense against Satan's plots, and so on. This imbalance is bad for two reasons. First, it means that science will remain rooted in the same old ideas and concepts rather than moving forward into new realms for the benefit of mankind. Even if we create spaceships or cure diseases, spiritually unhealthy mankind will still be miserable and misguided no matter how materially wealthy it may be. Indeed, our material wealth might actually make us miserable rather than happy! Thus, we need to research spiritual matters in order to ensure our minds and our spirits do not lag behind our bodies in their development. Secondly, an imbalance between science and spirituality might actually lead to the destruction of our species. Even without the interference of Satan– which is very significant indeed–too much advancement in the physical sciences could lead to the development of terrible weapons capable of killing us all.

> "The day science begins to study non-physical phenomena, it will make more progress in one decade than in all the previous centuries of its existence" – Nikola Tesla

A spiritually wise people would know never to use those sorts of weapons–like nuclear bombs–but humans as we now lack that wisdom. Thus, we run the risk of foolishly starting a great conflict that could destroy humanity entirely. The only way to avoid this is to spend as much time on spiritual research as we do on technical research, increasing our moral strength so that we only use physical technologies for good rather than self-aggrandizement.

The Power of Man and the Dichotomy of the Last Days

We might not be able to directly compete with angels and demons yet, but it is obvious we human beings are the most powerful living creatures on Earth. No other species is capable of as much virtue or as much destruction as we are. This is why all human beings, every one of us as individuals, are so dangerous. This includes you!

It is therefore easy to see why both Light and Dark are battling so fiercely for your soul. As a member of the highest species on Earth, you have a mandate for dominion across this entire planet. No animal or plant can fail to submit to you. Thus, God is looking for men and women to follow His example, as Jesus Christ did, and embody altruism and charity to strengthen the Light. By the same token, Satan wants humans, as rulers of Earth, to submit to him directly so that his plans can come to fruition on the most important planet of all—and if they do not, he is perfectly willing to destroy everyone and everything purely out of spite.

As we are living in the last days before the final battle, it is obvious there is a great dichotomy between two groups of people in the world today. This dichotomy exemplifies the dual opposition between honesty and dishonesty, truth and deceit. Satan's forces, who oppose human liberation, will generally try to bring lies and deception to the forefront. These Dark ones will be aided by those who primarily wish to defend and preserve their own lives, and also ensure humanity's consciousness remains limited. They are so trapped by the spiritual Matrix that even if they do not support Satan directly, it would be too psychologically devastating for them to liberate mankind.

In other words, the leadup to the final battle—the battle before the battle, so to speak—will be between truth seekers/truth bringers who wish to expose the truth, showing it to as many people as possible–and those who wish to preserve lies and keep as many of their fellow human beings in ignorance and unconsciousness as possible, preventing them from overcoming their limits. Keep in mind the saying, "there are none so blind as those who cannot see." This means that people who are wedded to denial, who refuse to see spiritual truths even when teachers, preachers, and enlightened beings lay it out for them in the simplest terms, are often the most dangerous soldiers in Satan's army, whether they realize it or not.

HOW TO RECOGNISE THE MATRIX AND FREE YOURSELF

"For we do not wrestle against flesh and blood, but against the rulers, against the authorities, against the cosmic powers over this present darkness, against the spiritual forces of evil in the heavenly places. 13 Therefore take up the whole armor of God, that you may be able to withstand in the evil day, and having done all, to stand firm." (English Standard Version, 2001, Ephesians 6:12-14).

These words apply to the spiritual Matrix that surrounds us right at this very moment. It isn't a literal veil you can touch, and you certainly can't rip it open with even the largest or sharpest knife. Just as the Bible says, it is a spiritual force, which means only spiritual methods can help you see beyond it. This chapter will detail a selection of such methods you can use to gain enlightenment, which will help you help others when the time of the final battle has arrived.

The Matrix we are in right now, just like the Matrix in the Hollywood movie, has completely shaped our perception of the world. That's what makes it so difficult to overcome, and it's understandable why so few, even among the most educated, have been unable to do so. Thus, you should not feel bad if even now you feel as if you cannot resist it. Given that you're inside of it, for all your life it has been the only thing you could touch, taste, smell, hear, and feel. It is your only reference point for anything.

As Morpheus said to Neo,

> **Morpheus**: *The Matrix is everywhere. It is all around us. Even now, in this very room. You can see it when you look out your window or when you turn on your television. You can feel it when you go to work... when you go to church... when you pay your taxes. It is the world that has been pulled over your eyes to blind you from the truth.*

> **Neo**: *What truth?*

Morpheus: *That you are a slave, Neo. Like everyone else, you were born into bondage. Into a prison that you cannot taste or see or touch. A prison for your mind." - Lana Wachowski*

So how could you be expected to tell what is true and what is false?

The answer is training. You can train yourself, through conscious mental effort, to go beyond the false illusions the spiritual Matrix inflicts on you, and raise your mind to an awareness of the spiritual realities it keeps from you, even if you cannot separate yourself from it entirely until and unless Light wins the spiritual war–which we will discuss in the next chapter. In other words, you can 'be in the Matrix, but not of the Matrix'.

Morpheus was explaining how awareness is a very subtle thing. Even though you might not be able to put it into words, the fact that you can tell something is off about the world makes you more enlightened than others. That is the very first step you must take. Listen to the little voice deep inside of yourself. That is your connection to the Universal Father Himself. When you are listening to that little voice, also think about who you are as a person. What are your greatest hopes, dreams, and goals? What do you value? What do you seek to avoid? What kinds of people are most important to you—in other words, who are your friends and family?

As you get more familiar with yourself and understand the world around you as well as your place in it, you will then start to wonder about larger, deeper questions. You will want to know the true nature of your existence, what it means to exist in this world, what the purpose of your existence is, and what your reason for being alive is.

The dark brothers and sisters have done a wonderful job of keeping all Humans in darkness for a long time. They believe that their world (Matrix) is all you deserve. It is so easy to brush it off and forget that we are part of this Matrix. Matrix pumps so much into our heads, that we humans are wired to accept it as a reality. Our brain has been hooked onto the feed from the Matrix, hooked for years and years, hooked real bad.

> "It is so easy to forget how much noise Matrix pumps into your head until you unplug." – Matrix4

But,

some part of you knows this (life in Matrix) is not your real life

Some part of you remembers what is real

Some part of you remembers what life is like outside the Matrix

Some part of you know what freedom looks like

Some part of you know what a world without controls looks like

Some part of you can feel this (life outside Matrix) as a real memory

Depending on your Soul purpose and experience, when the time is right, you will begin to ask questions, and you will start to grow in awareness; this will ultimately drive you to become a truth-seeker, which itself leads to becoming a truth-bringer. All you have to do, as Morpheus might say, is 'follow the white rabbit" to the path of freedom and enlightenment.

STAGE IS SET - FINAL BATTLE FOR PLANET EARTH HAS BEGUN

"God's laser focus is on Earth and humanity; this is where all the action of the universe is. Many big shots from across the multiverse are gathered and watching intently the chess games between Light and Dark on planet Earth." - Trinity Royal

The curtain is rising on the greatest show the entire universe- not just Earth-has ever seen. Armed with the info you have now, you are in the front seat.

You now behold a great battlefield where two armies are facing off against each other, each of which is trillions upon trillions of soldiers strong. One of these armies consists

of golden spirits bathed in heavenly alabaster light. At its head is the banner of Christ, or Jesus as he was known on earth: A set of three concentric azure circles on a pure white background. The other army is made up of horrifying monsters and shadowy beings. At the head of this army is the most powerful monster of them all, the fallen angel Lucifer aided by his trump card Satan, determined to enslave all of creation, and mire the entire universe in darkness for all eternity. Lucifer carries his own banner. It has a white background, like that of Light, but in its center is a single red circle, and in the center of that is a single solid black circle. It looks like a terrible eye; some seekers might compare it to the eye of Sauron from the Lord of the Rings movie trilogy. Many times even entertainment can reveal hidden spiritual truths, for just like Sauron in Tolkien's books, Lucifer is a cruel and ruthless dominator who wants to control everyone and everything else.

These two armies of Light and Dark are utterly dwarfed by the spectators surrounding them. A great throng of angels in the entire universe is watching the confrontation intently. But the real center of attention is between those two massive armies. Both of them are vying for a single small ball of rock—a pale blue dot, as Carl Sagan might say. On this pale blue dot live billions of humble material creatures, evolved throughout millions of years, the vast majority of which are completely unaware of the struggle being waged around them and their central significance to it.

You guessed right—that pale blue dot is Earth, and its residents, human beings–including you and me–are the true prize of this conflict. The forces of Light, led by Christ in his human form as Jesus Christ, want the best for humanity. They want us to liberate ourselves from the Matrix which keeps us ignorant of spiritual warfare and higher realities so that our souls can ascend to Heaven and reach closer and closer to God. Lucifer's army wants to enslave us or annihilate us if that is not possible. He wants to stunt our spiritual development and keep us blind, miserable, and in perpetual conflict with each other. While the Light gains energy from human beings purifying their souls, ascending to higher vibratory planes after death, and turning evil to good, the Dark gains energy from trapping souls in the material universe forever, so their negative emotions can be used as batteries powering Lucifer's evil plans.

The chess games between both factions are keeping this planet in a stalemate. There are so many things that both factions do behind the scenes that we rarely know or hear about. Secrecy is also maintained for a reason. According to higher consciousness beings, Humans are on the way and getting close to becoming part of light brotherhood/sisterhood. This status has to be achieved, it cannot be given. The amount of light quotient the species/planet generates is the deciding factor. The human species at this time is teetering on the edges of being accepted into the greater destiny. Dark forces are very aware and they have their own plans.

We will draw one more analogy as this book comes to a close. The increase in war, violence, and suffering we see today can be compared to a mother's birthing pains. In this case, we are speaking of Mother Earth herself, or our entire planet considered as a whole. The mother waits for contractions, several stages must progress, and then the actual labor itself begins. Contractions, the water breaking, and all that are necessary prerequisites for birth. By the same token, the chaos we see today, as difficult as it may be to endure, is a necessary precondition for the birth of a brand-new world after the final battle has been won and the spiritual Matrix has been shattered.

As the curtain rises, the great angel Gabriel, known popularly as the messenger of the highest; who is also the executive assistant to Christ in the Universal realms has blown the trumpet.

The eyes of the entire universe are on Earth—and YOU, specifically! God and all of His creations are paying very close attention to your choices and actions. However, they are absolutely not judging you one way or the other—you are perfectly free to make all of your own choices. The real question is how the show is going to end. Who will eventually win the great spiritual war of the ages, Light or Darkness?

The choice always was and always will be yours. How will you respond?

Conclusion

I f you have read this book, my friend, you are ready for the next steps. Even if you do not yet believe, however, the fact that you are even reading this book to the end proves that you are a genuine seeker of truth. So in that respect, the only thing I ask of you is to keep your eyes and mind open. Pay close attention to the people and situations around you and in the world. Be very conscious of your emotional state, and very mindful of the effect your actions have on others. Don't overlook even small details that might not have any significance at first glance. And most of all, think critically about the messages you see on TV, on the Internet, and in any other kind of mass media. In most cases, the truth is behind the words.

This is just good advice in general even if you're still skeptical about spiritual matters, you will live a happier life by following it. But if you are willing to think deeply about why such advice is good, you will find yourself tumbling down a rabbit hole that leads you to worlds beyond this one and a reality far greater than basic materialism could give you.

As Morpheus might say, you have already taken the red pill. You now just need to accept it.

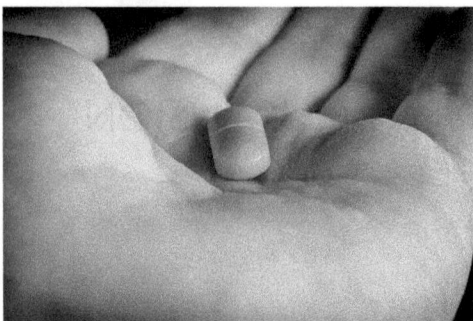

Thank You

I want to personally Thank you for reading this book.

This is my best book. I have poured my Heart and Soul into these pages. I hope you have gained some valuable insights from the information presented. Please consider leaving your valuable review. Your review and feedback are important to me. Thank you so much.

★ ★ ★ ★ ★

Scan to leave review:

Scripture verses Related to War in Heaven

[Revelation 12:7-10] War broke out in heaven. Michael and his angels fought against the dragon, and the dragon and his angels fought back. 8 But he was not strong enough, and they lost their place in heaven.

[Revelation 12:9] And the great dragon was cast out, that old serpent, called the Devil, and Satan, which deceiveth the whole world: he was cast out into the earth, and his angels were cast out with him. [Revelation 12:12] Therefore rejoice, ye heavens, and ye that dwell in them. Woe to the inhabiters of the earth and of the sea! for the devil is come down unto you, having great wrath, because he knoweth that he hath but a short time.

[Isaiah 14:12] How art thou fallen from heaven, O Lucifer, son of the morning! how art thou cut down to the ground, which didst weakens the nations!

[Daniel 12:1] And at that time shall Michael stand up, the great prince which standeth for the children of thy people: and there shall be a time of trouble, such as never was since there was a nation even to that same time: and at that time thy people shall be delivered, every one that shall be found written in the book.

[Isaiah 14:13-14] You said in your heart, "I will ascend to the heavens; I will raise my throne above the stars of God; I will sit enthroned on the mount of assembly, on the utmost heights of Mount Zaphon. I will ascend above the tops of the clouds; I will make myself like the Most High.

[Revelation9:1] And the fifth angel sounded, and I saw a star fall from heaven unto the earth: and to him was given the key of the bottomless pit

[Ephesians 6:10-18] Finally, be strong in the Lord and in the strength of his might. Put on the whole armor of God, so that you may be able to stand against the schemes of the devil. For we do not wrestle against flesh and blood, but against the rulers, against the authorities, against the cosmic powers over this present darkness, against the spiritual forces of evil in the heavenly places. Therefore take up the whole armor of God, that you may be able to withstand in the evil day, and having done all, to stand firm. Stand therefore, having fastened on the belt of truth, and having put on the breastplate of righteousness in place, and with your feet fitted with the readiness that comes from the gospel of peace. In addition to all this, take up the shield of faith, with which you can extinguish all the flaming arrows of the evil one. Take the helmet of salvation and the sword of the Spirit, which is the word of God.

[John 10:10] The thief comes only to steal and kill and destroy. I came that they may have life and have it abundantly.

[Revelation 20:8] And will come out to deceive the nations that are at the four corners of the earth, Gog and Magog, to gather them for battle; their number is like the sand of the sea.

[Mathew 4:3] And the tempter came and said to him, "If you are the Son of God, command these stones to become loaves of bread."

[Mathew 4:1] Then Jesus was led up by the Spirit into the wilderness to be tempted by the devil.

[Exodus 15:3] The Lord is a warrior; the Lord is his name"

[Genesis 6:1-4] When man began to multiply on the face of the land and daughters were born to them, the sons of God saw that the daughters of man were attractive. And they took as their wives any they chose. Then the Lord said, "My Spirit shall not abide in man forever, for he is flesh: his days shall be 120 years." The Nephilim were on the earth in those days, and also afterward, when the sons of God came in to the daughters of man and they bore children to them. These were the mighty men who were of old, the men of renown.

[Ezekiel 28:15] You (referring to Lucifer) were blameless in your ways from the day you were created till wickedness was found in you.

[Ezekiel 28:17] Your (referring to Lucifer) heart was proud because of your beauty; you corrupted your wisdom for the sake of your splendor. I cast you to the ground; I exposed you before kings, to feast their eyes on you.

[Ezekiel 28:14] You (referring to Lucifer) were the anointed guardian cherub. I placed you; you were on the holy mountain of God; in the midst of the stones of fire you walked.

PREVIEW FROM BOOK2: THE REAL REASONS FOR SECOND COMING OF CHRIST

T he curtain has risen and the spotlight is on you. But the show hasn't gotten to the climax just yet. Both you and the audience are waiting for one more person to show up, the most important of all. It is one man, born two thousand and twenty-two years ago, at the time of this writing. The entire multiverse has been waiting with bated breath for Him to make His reappearance, and it is almost time.

You guessed right: That being is Jesus Christ. The great Christ is not going to sit out the final battle with Darkness. Still, in his persona as Jesus, given through Bestowal, he will lead the forces of Light when the day finally comes. He comes as a warrior.

If enough human beings have empowered the Light through personal enlightenment, practicing divine virtues like love and altruism, and ascending their souls to higher vibratory levels; this will make the job much easier for the Light, that is why it is so important to do everything you can in service to the Light.

Even if this were not the final battle, and Christ was returning in more peaceful times, it would still be the most unique event in the history of the entire multiverse. No other planet in any other galaxy in the multiverse has had as much of a direct connection to the divine as ours does.

This will be the ONLY planet in the Universe to have its creator walk the second time. Christ was the only being to be born as a helpless baby, grow up as a mortal, and then complete his mission to deny Satan—once, and then subsequently agree to return a second time to the world to complete the removal and dissolution of Matrix. Even the Universal Father Himself has never enacted a plan like that; it is a very new thing for Him as well. Humans are creating a history that will be told for all generations in the universe.

However, it should be noted that the decade 2020s is crucial for the battle. This has been foreseen 200,000 years ago. Lots and lots of preparation have gone in for thousands of years for this exact moment in time for both factions. All the critical higher-level beings that are battle-tested in this epic war, both dark and light are born in the world today, although most may not know it consciously. Higher-level beings who have chosen to be part of this battle are present today. Some are activated and the vast majority are asleep and or devoured by the illusions of the Matrix.

<snip...>

If you like this preview, you will absolutely love Book-2 of 'The Real Matrix'. I highly recommend this one.

Lucifer Rebellion. Christ vs Satan – The Second Coming of Christ

Scan Me

Ever wonder **why there is a War between GOD and Devil?**

Ever wonder how the **War in Heaven started or what Lucifer Rebellion is**? **and why War in Heaven came to Earth** and why darkness still exists on Earth?

This book explores:

- How and Why did the **war in Heaven start**?

- How did the War in Heaven come to Earth?

- Why did **God send Christ** to planet Earth? Was it to save Humanity and the Universe?

- What are the effects of War on Earth and in Heaven?

- What exactly happened during **Christ's First Coming** event?

- What is expected during the Second Coming event?

I invite you to join me on a journey beyond space and time when the Lucifer Rebellion started and the reasons for Christ's First and Second Coming events.

Christ & Demons - Unseen Realms of Darkness

"The reason the Son of God appeared was to destroy the Devil's work." -Ephesians 6:12

Is there an **UNSEEN world of Darkness** hidden in front of our eyes?

Ever wonder why **Evil** exists on Earth? Ever wonder how **Satan got to planet Earth a**nd what exactly is the Dark Empire Agenda?

Ever wonder why Christ chose planet Earth for His great Bestowal?

What is the **agenda of Darkness**? Why do God and Christ let dark forces flourish on Earth? Does God have a plan? What is it?

What are the differences between **Demons, Evil Spirits, and Ghosts**? How does **Selling one's Soul to the devil** happen?

Son of Man becomes Son of God. One Event that Changed the History of the World

<u>Award-Winning Book</u>

"an opportunity for the reader to embark on a journey with Him, feel what He feels"

"A fascinating description and story of how Christ emerged, changed and developed into the highest of holiest beings, second only to God."

"An exceptional and well-written novel without the preaching and pointless prose and verbiage of others of this type"

There is **ONE event** that is the true turning point in the history of Earth. This is not the Birth or Baptism of Jesus, but it is the **fight with the Devil**

Ever wonder what would have happened to Earth if Christ failed against Satan?
This was a real possibility, although it is considered blasphemous to talk about it.

What Happened on Easter Saturday? 36 hr mystery between Death and Resurrection

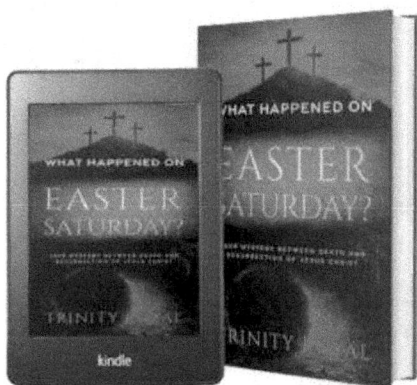

Scan Me

"A five-star read, absolutely."

"It stands to reason that Saturday was a critical time for Him"

"I highly recommend this incredible book as it takes the reader through both the physical and spiritual journey of Him as he underwent His transformation. **A five-star read, absolutely**."

"I for one never really thought about that Saturday, so for me **it was a riveting experience**, learning about that previously overlooked time."

Ever wonder **what happened when Christ was inside the Tomb for 36 hrs** between death and resurrection?

Ever wonder **what body did Christ have after Resurrection**? and why the **resurrection process take 3 days?** why not 1-day or 2-days?

Welcome to Heaven. Your Graduation from Kindergarten Earth to Heaven

"I go and prepare a place for you, I will come back and take you to be with me that you also may be where I am." - John 14:3

Ever wonder **if Heaven is real**? What **proof** do we have?

How does one **go to Heaven**? What are the **minimum requirements for Heaven**?

Why **_Life of Earth is your Kindergarten school_**?

Trinity explores the following:

- Isn't Heaven **just a mind concept**? *What is the proof of its existence? Why do I even bother about Heaven? What is in it for me?*

- What are the **minimum requirements to go to Heaven or the ticket booth to Heaven**?

- Why is life on Earth your **kindergarten school**?

- Are there **different levels to heaven? If so, how many? What are they?** Does the **time and space continuum exist in Heaven?** *If so how different is it compared to Earth's time and space?*

Your Life in Heaven. Family, Marriage, Sex, Work

"No eye has seen, no ear has heard, and no mind has imagined what God has prepared for those who love him." – 1 Corinthians 2:9

Ever wonder what your **life in Heaven will look like after your mortal death**?

Is there **Marriage** in Heaven? Do you have a **Family in Heaven**?

Do you have your **Parents or kids or your siblings** in Heaven?

Do you have **Sexual intercourse** in Heaven?

And what do you do all day? Is there a **daily Job**? Oh. And will you meet your **deceased family members**, friends, and relatives?

These are questions that curious minds like me ask. You will find **authoritative un-speculated** answers here.

SOS - Save yOur Soul

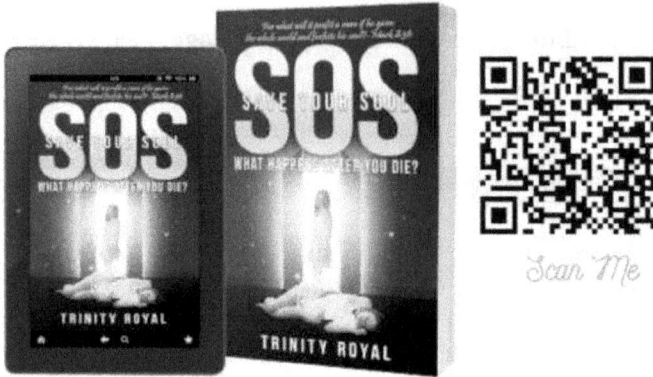

"For what shall it profit a man, if he shall gain the whole world, and lose his own soul?" - *Mark* 8:36

Ever Wonder **What Happens After You Die**? Is it the end?

What did **Christ** Say about death and life after mortal death?

Is there a way to Save yOur Soul? If so How?

What exactly is **Soul** and **Spirit**, is it just a new age concept? What did Christ Say?

Trinity considered to be one of the bridges between Heaven and Earth, shares general Angelic knowledge. This book explores:

What are the unseen parts of us that make us who we are? What is left behind after Mortal death and what happens to these **unseen parts of us**?

What exactly is **Soul** and **Spirit**, is it just a new age concept? What did Christ Say? Is there a way to Save yOur Soul? If so How? Does Heaven actually exist? Can a ticket to Heaven be guaranteed?

From Suffering to Healing

"I highly recommend this for anyone *who has ever suffered in their lives*, and, in all honesty, who hasn't?"

Why do **bad things happen to good people**?

Why does your **Life journey lead you to suffer?**

The Answer is to Heal You.

Your suffering is the epitome of a **blessing in disguise.** Wrapped in darkness and suffering, it removes the ground from beneath your feet and leaves you fearful, fragile, and devoid of meaning in life.

Most beings that we adore or worship have gone through dark times in their life. This includes Christ, Buddha, Gandhi, Nelson Mandela, Oprah, Abraham Lincoln, etc. This process is necessary as it redefines a person, re-makes one character, and chips away the darkness to bring out the luster of your **Real Self.** This is your **METAMORPHOSIS.**

Award-Winning Book

Our wounds are often the openings into the best and the most beautiful parts of us." -David Richo

Ever wonder **why suffering happens for no known reason...**

Ever wonder **why your Soul is longing...**

Have you ever felt like you have a **splinter in your mind, that does not let you off the hook..**

If so, **you are chosen for a purpose. There is GOD's hand working in your life.**

While there are many reasons people suffer (most are self-made or bad decisions or external in nature); the type of Suffering referred to as the "Dark Night
of the Soul" has a clear and definite purpose. **The purpose is your Soul's growth.**

Your Answers and Healing await. Click on Buy Now.

Special Bonus - Free books to our readers

Free books to our readers

War in Heaven came to Earth. Satan Rebellion:

https://dl.bookfunnel.com/ea12ys3dmk

Your Life in Heaven:

https://dl.bookfunnel.com/vg451qpuzs

REFERENCES

References

English Standard Version Bible. (2001). ESV Online.

The Jesusonian Foundation. (2021). The Urantia Book. TruthBook.

Cairnes, Julie Von Nonveiller. (2019, September 15). The Battle be- tween Light and Dark.

h t t p s : / / m e d i u m . com/spiritual-warfare-the-new-predator/the-battle-between-light- and-dark-7bbccbeba738 – Medium, Spiritual Warfare & The New Predator.

Candace Letters - https://Abundanthope.net

The Jesusonian Foundation. (2022, May 4). The Urantia Book. Truth-Book

Quotes reference – Matrix movie series

About Author

Trinity is a multi-award-winning author and a spiritual warrior. While life might not always work out according to plan, Trinity was able to take valuable lessons from each new experience. Trinity grew and developed and now shares a passion for enlightening others on spiritual knowledge in the hopes of closing the gap between Heaven and Earth. Trinity's writings reflect the depths of a passion and desire to connect with everyone seeking spiritual growth and education.

You can learn more at www.RocketshipPath2God.com or @ https://www.facebook.com/TrinityRoyalBooks